VERMONT
Portrait of the Land and Its People

by George Wuerthner and Mollie Yoneko Matteson

© American Geographic Publishing
Helena, Montana

William A. Cordingley, Chairman
Rick Graetz, Publisher
Mark Thompson, Director of Publications
Barbara Fifer, Assistant Book Editor

ACKNOWLEDGMENTS AND DEDICATION

No project of this breadth could have been accomplished without the invaluable contributions of many people and sources. A number of previously published books and reports were of immeasurable help in the compilation of this text, but several titles were particularly useful and readers of this book may wish to consult them for greater depth of information. These books include: Charles Johnson's *The Nature of Vermont,* Harold Meeks' *Time and Change in Vermont—A Human Geography,* and Charles Morrissey's *Vermont—A History.* In addition, numerous individuals shared their knowledge and impressions of the state—too many to list here by name—but their love of Vermont, which was freely shared, is gratefully acknowledged.

Finally, this work would not have come to fruition without the generous support of Robert and Mary Matteson of Bennington, who shared their perspectives on Vermont politics and history as well as providing their Shaftsbury farmhouse as a base of operations during the months of research. To them this book is respectfully dedicated.

Library of Congress Cataloging in Publication Data
Wuerthner, George.
 Vermont, portrait of the land and its people.

 (American geographic series)
 Summary: Surveys the history, geography, geology, climate, and plant and animal life of Vermont.
 1. Vermont—Description and travel—Juvenile literature. 2. Vermont—History—Juvenile literature. [1. Vermont] I. Matteson, Mollie Yoneko. II. Title. III. Series.
F49.3.W84 1987 974.3 87-19527
ISBN 0-938314-39-4 (pbk.)

ISBN 0-938314-39-4

© 1987 American Geographic Publishing
Box 5630, Helena, MT 59604
(406) 443-2842

Text © 1987 George Wuerthner and Mollie Yoneko Matteson

Design by Len Visual Design; Linda Collins, graphic artist.
Printed in Hong Kong by DNP America, Inc., San Francisco

CONTENTS

Photos: Title page, Lake Rescue. SONJA BULLATY
Facing page: South Saxtons River, Grafton. JAMES RANDKLEV
Left: Newfane. ROBERT PERRON

Front cover photos, left top: On Mt. Mansfield. IMAGERY
Bottom: Marble quarry. BULLATY-LOMEO
Right: East Orange in autumn light. JEFF GNASS

Back cover photos, top: The Mad River Valley. FRANK BALTHIS
Bottom. Showy ladyslipper. TED LEVIN

ABOUT THE AUTHORS

Mollie Yoneko Matteson was raised in Bennington, Vermont where her family's roots go back to the first white settlers of the region. She has worked as a wilderness ranger for the U.S. Forest Service in Montana and Wyoming as well as for the National Park Service in Washington and the Vermont State Parks department.

Writer-photographer-naturalist George Wuerthner has been employed as a university instructor in California, a surveyor in Wyoming, a wilderness ranger in Alaska and a botanist in Idaho. He has backpacked, skied, kayaked and canoed extensively in wild places from Mexico to Alaska. His writing and photography have appeared in many natural history and outdoor publications and he has written two books in the American Geographic Series.

FOREWORD

"Little Rhody" is nearly forgotten. Some mornings I take a run down the old woods road, soft with the molding leaves of many autumns, and slow or even stop at the small cemetery. In the deep shade of several large white pines, I have to strain to read the names on the eroded marble headstones. It is startling, no matter how many times I wander down here. There is my name, "Matteson," carved and echoing silently from dozens of leaning, broken stones. I usually do not linger. In the still, dim forest, it is unnerving to meet such a density of relatives.

They came from Rhode Island in the latter half of the 18th century and settled this valley a few miles west of the steep slopes of Glastenbury Mountain— hence "Little Rhody." It wasn't prime land; the valley is swampy and the ground is more rock than soil. The weather can test anyone's stamina, and 200 years ago the long, damp winters and rainy, muddy springs taxed more than just mental well-being. But the pioneers determined to make this inhuman land habitable anyway, clearing the trees, piling rocks up as walls between fields, building, damming, planting.

In such a place, the past permeated my childhood. I took much of it for granted, growing up with a 260-year-old farmhouse as a weekend retreat, looking up daily at the Bennington Battle Monument as I walked to school. Many native Vermonters, I think, possess this kind of easy acceptance of antiquities and historical markers that recent migrants or tourists find significant and remarkable, (or believe they should). As a young girl, I liked covered bridges— those darlings of the postcard photographers— inasmuch as they were too narrow for more than one car to pass through them at a time. Whenever we approached one, I experienced a surge of excitement: would there be an oncoming car at the other entrance? Would we have a head-on in the middle of the old Silk Road Bridge?

But unlike increasing numbers of young Vermonters, I grew up where my own genealogy has entangled itself about the land for better than two centuries. For a child, living where your ancestors live— where lots of dead people related to you used to live— accords intrigue to otherwise mundane places and events. There was a thrill in seeing my family name on dozens of headstones, in three different cemeteries, each Memorial Day. I felt a mild smugness creep over me each time we drove "Matteson Road." And the Peter Matteson Tavern Museum— well of course in some indirect way I deserved credit for this too.

The feeling is probably the same wherever families have lived for generations. Your name on other people and places verifies your existence; they capture your attention and confirm your presence the same way a glimpse of yourself reflected in a store window is a slightly startling reminder that you are indeed "real" and not just a figment of your own imagination.

Even for those who did not grow up in Vermont, living here can be a process of self-validation. With just more than half a million residents, each individual counts. Government, both physically and politically, is easily accessible to those who wish to participate. In Vermont, too, there is a tradition of public use of private land that allows even those who are not landowners easy access to outdoor recreation in the meadows and forests. During the deer season, hunters stroll the old logging road and crisscross the woods on my family's property; in winter, snowmobile tracks stripe our fields. Although I have always harbored my own reservations (preferring hiking to hunting, and cross-country skiing to 'biling), my father in the Yankee tradition has never questioned or resented it. And for myself, I grew up without fear of barbed wire fences and boundary markers. So long as I do not tread impolitely close to someone's home, I often ignore "no trespassing" signs, taking them for mere formalities. I am also as outraged as any deer hunter when a crude or ignorant property owner bars me from walking through his woods.

The Vermont landscape itself is comfortable and human-scale, not overwhelming in size or spectacle. After living in the West for several years, I have encountered numerous people who say to me, after I tell them I was raised in Vermont: "Oh, yes! I hear it's really beautiful there." It is hard to respond appropriately, when we are surrounded by 10,000'-high snow-draped mountains, or are only a stone's throw from some vast, pristine wilderness area. "Beautiful? Ah, yes, it is quite nice," I say, feeling slightly disloyal, but not wanting to mislead someone who's hardly ever been a hundred miles east of the Continental Divide.

But Vermont, unlike many parts of the country (including the wide-open West), wears the marks of humanity well. Some say that the scenery is even enhanced by the close conjunction of humans and nature. Vermont is neither wilderness nor inner city, nor a worst-of-both-worlds suburbia, and there are few places where the blend of man and land is so visually, and philosophically, appealing. The mix of mountains, meadows, farms and villages seems as close to a true, benevolent partnership of wild and civilized as there can be anywhere. Even Vermont's larger communities— tucked into river valleys, set in wide basins, fronted by blue lakes or backed by forested slopes— seem to be graced, not resented, by the natural landscape.

I never truly appreciated this particular quality of the Green Mountain state until I travelled to the West as an adult. Cities, it goes without saying, are places where human influence is total. But even in other rural regions, people and land looked more as if they were at war, or at best, had struck an unhappy truce. The checkerboard farmlands of the Midwest, the geometric mono-croplands of California's Great Central Valley: Man had been too heavyfisted, the land too passive. And in the mountains, both the abandoned and the surviving mining towns seemed weary of the struggle to drag life from hard rock. If the effort had not lasted too long or been too harsh, the rivers and forests might eventually heal themselves.

But perhaps because Vermont's scenery depends so heavily on a fine balance of natural and man-made features, even minor human excesses can be glaring insults to the sensitive eye. Tourists may avert their glance, residents may ignore or tune them out, but mobile homes and leaning, decaying shacks dot the Green Mountains, in places as densely as any in southern Appalachia. Roadside gravel pits, murky streams and dingy, slightly tinted air demonstrate that purity is not ubiquitous. Sited next to a 19th-century New England village, a concrete shopping mall may seem indecent, or even criminal. And the resorts and ski areas, posh and tidy though they may be, ring hollow to many Vermonters. In Sherburne or Ludlow, Waitsfield or Stowe, the rows of cedar-shake condos; the giant supermarkets selling fresh pasta and strange, imported fruits; the inevitable Tyrolian lodges and Ye Olde Pubs— beneath the shiny surface runs a disturbing, almost sinister current. It flows, it seems, from some removed, distant power that cares not for any place in particular, but merely for the broadening of its empire.

Vermont's basic racial homogeneity— despite the French Canadians, Italians, Irish and other immigrant groups that are, in any case, still all Caucasian— is one reason for the relative absence of strong class and social tensions. In my town, as throughout most of the state, a black or Asian person was a curiosity, and usually attracted attention, not animosity. All during my childhood, my own mixed background of Japanese and old Yankee WASP prompted uninhibited schoolmates to ask: "What are you anyway? Indian?" Or, "Are you one of those boat people?" My mother wouldn't have liked

The 18th-century Peter Matteson tavern near Shaftsbury.
GEORGE WUERTHNER

it, but I was often tempted to say yes.

Racial sameness thus has its benefits, even for those few who are different. But it can also breed an ignorant and provincial populace, with little understanding of the complex, often destructive social dynamics outside this quiet kingdom.

Although the diversity and liveliness of the city is attractive to many young Vermonters, a few find the state too tame in other ways. There are no great tracts of wildland here, and almost every acre, even in official wilderness areas, has been touched and modified in some way by human hands. When I was 16, I climbed to the summit of Bald Mountain west of Bennington and was completely unprepared for the eastward view of unbroken forest; I had never seen anything like it. Later, I read that that this is one of the most extensive views of undeveloped terrain in the state.

And despite Vermont's acclaimed natural beauty, that which truly animates a landscape— wildlife— is neither very abundant nor diverse. Even the white-tailed deer, which is the only species some Vermonters think of when one mentions the word "wildlife," is rare enough that I have never seen but one (living that is) in all the years I have lived here. Black bears, moose and coyotes we have in some number, but these too are seen infrequently. Chipmunks and woodchucks living under the shed may satisfy some wildlife watchers, but I find the Green Mountains dishearteningly still. Natural history accounts are particularly troubling— the panther or catamount, the wolf, the pine marten all are gone, and others like the Atlantic salmon, river otter and common loon are present in pitifully low numbers.

Since the early 1800s, not more than a generation or two since those first pioneers came to the region, young Vermonters have looked elsewhere to fulfill their dreams. While the state's population has grown considerably in the last two decades after more than a century of stagnation and decline, the in-migration of non-natives mostly accounts for this rise. The newcomers have been attracted to Vermont largely because it seems "stuck in time," and indeed it was for quite an extended period. But this very quality, which is actually diminishing around the state as development spreads, also sends young natives away. While their sense of place may be strong, may even be rooted by many previous generations of Vermonters, the adventurous and the ambitious often move on. And those who remain have little desire to preserve Vermont as a pastoral parkland or sleepy, wayside province. They demand that the jobs and the amenities of modern life be brought to them. Undeniably, that is happening.

But few who grow up here, whether they stay or migrate elsewhere, can or want to entirely shake the Green Mountain State from their identity. Vermont fosters loyalty in anyone who knows it, whether or not he was born here. Developer or preservationist, industrialist or environmentalist, young millworker or retired urban escapee, all share a sense that there is something different, something Vermont-y about Vermont, that is worth keeping. It is an ideal of community and familiarity, a manageable and comforting scale of both human and natural things, land- and townscapes that are aesthetically pleasing and perhaps most important though the hardest to grasp— a sense that here is a place that not only allows the individual to participate in the present, but also reaffirms his connections to the past and his valid existence in the world.

Mollie Yoneko Matteson
Shaftsbury, Vermont
May 1987

CHAPTER ONE

GREEN MOUNTAIN STATE

In a mythical kingdom called Vermont, there are rolling, verdant hills dotted with red barns, and snug villages with Christmas-card charisma and soaring, slender white church steeples. It is thought this land is inhabited by independent men and women, stubborn survivors of a rocky, unyielding environment. While many left this place for more bounteous provinces, those who were loyal to their ancestors' ground drew psychological sustenance from a strong sense of community and a belief in individual worth and import— or so the legend goes.

Like all myths of a place and a people, the conception of Vermont as an agrarian, participatory democracy sheltered in a still-unruined nook of the Northeast contains a kernel of truth. It once was remarkably close to that ideal image. And although today the reality is rapidly changing, it changes in part because these stories and the visions of Vermont still are dynamic elements of its persona. The myth is perpetuated— in magazines, promotional brochures, coffee table picture books— and lives even yet in the hearts of longtime residents who should know better.

The truth is that Vermont is a small piece of land; with an area of 9,609 square miles, Vermont ranks 43rd in size among the 50 states. Among the six New England states, however, it is second largest after Maine. Shaped vaguely like a human footprint, the southern end (or the narrow "heel") abuts northern Massachusetts, and is only 40.5 miles wide, while the northern boundary— shared with the Canadian province of Quebec— is 90 miles wide. Its greatest length, north to south, is 157.5 miles, but both the east and west borderlines are considerably longer as they follow the wriggling water bodies on either side— the Connecticut River on the east margin and Lake Champlain on the western edge.

Within this compact space live an estimated 535,000 people (1985 figures) which means only Alaska and Wyoming have smaller populations. But even the 49th and 50th ranked states have a big city or two. Alaska, for example, has Anchorage, a town of some quarter million souls. Vermont has no major urban areas and the populace is more or less evenly distributed over the state. Its communities are of pleasingly modest, human dimensions. Residents know their neighbors,

and citizens can participate directly in local government through the annual Town Meeting. Despite Vermont's small size, however, there remains a sense of space and distance. The suburban sprawl that infects so much of the East has not yet overtaken Vermont. The towns are still distinct, still separated by stretches of undeveloped landscape. As one Vermont schoolgirl wrote: "I like Vermont because the trees are close together and the people are far apart."

Above: Stickney Brook, Windham County. JAMES RANDKLEV

Facing page, right: In most people's minds Vermont is the epitome of America where independent, wholesome people live in tidy villages, such as here at Middletown Springs. GEORGE WUERTHNER

Left: TED LEVIN

Above: In 1850 an estimated 80 percent of Vermont was cleared for agricultural production, while today only 19 percent of the state is still farmed. Barn in Shaftsbury. GEORGE WUERTHNER

Facing page, left: One reason for the reduction in farm acres can be attributed to changing technology. The replacement of draft horses with tractors means fewer acres are planted with crops that in the past supported farm stock animals such as horses. BULLATY-LOMEO

Right: The short autumn foliage season attracts more than a million visitors to the state, and is the busiest time of year for the tourist industry. JAMES RANDKLEV

Most Rural

According to the U.S. Bureau of Census, Vermont is the most rural state in the union. While this seems to confirm the common belief that the state is dominantly agricultural, it is actually a misleading designation. Some 60 percent of Vermonters are considered rural "nonfarm" residents; in other words, they live in the country, but probably work in a nearby town. Or these back-road dwellers may write, weave tapestry or live off their investments. And most country dwellers must still orient their lives around some larger population center where they shop, go to the movies or to a restaurant, or just meet friends.

Even Vermont's major regional centers would bare-ly qualify as cities in other states. This, to outside observers at least, furthers the rustic image. Burlington, with a population of 38,000, is the largest community,

followed by Rutland (17,950), Bennington (16,131), Essex (14,590), Colchester (12,950), Brattleboro (12,025), South Burlington (11,000) and Springfield (10,140). All other towns have fewer than 10,000 people.

While most modern-day Vermonters do not live on working farms, the celebrated agrarian society was a reality in the state's past. The state flag is graced by a placid bovine, and one still hears the old saw about Vermont having more cows than people. Even in the heyday of dairying this was a bit of an exaggeration (the highest cow population ever was 290,000 in 1920, a year when humans totalled 352,000) but to be sure, the state was once almost entirely blanketed with fields and farms. In the 19th century approximately 80 percent of the state was cleared of trees for grazing and cultivation. Today the strength of this pastoral legacy is evident in, among other places, local bookstores. A recent quick scan through the titles in a shop's Vermont section showed that, without exception, every book featured a barn or other farm scene on its cover!

Most of the state's original settlers were farmers and thus landowners as well. By 1793 all Vermont land had been placed into private ownership. The landedness of the populace led, in turn, to another aspect of the Vermont ideal— that of equality and freedom. In the tradition of western civilization, stemming from the time of feudal Europe, land ownership was the prerequisite for citizenship. In the American colonies this custom was perpetuated, as the first state constitutions granted the right to vote only to landed men. Vermont's constitution, adopted in 1791, was the first to grant universal suffrage to all male residents (women would come later) and was the pioneer as well in officially outlawing the practice of slavery.

The number of farms and of cleared acres probably were at their maximum by 1850, but few statistics are available on the number of individual operations. The loss of topsoil due to overgrazing, along with the availability of more productive agricultural lands in the Midwest, resulted in a net out-migration of Vermonters seeking better lives elsewhere. In addition, the rise of the manufacturing industry in the state lured hillside farmers from their rocky fields to towns like Springfield and Bennington, where they worked for wages at the mills and shops.

In 1900 Vermont had 33,104 farms, but by 1987 this number had shrunk to 2,771. Meanwhile the average acreage per farm rose from 143 acres to more than 250. Today only 19 percent of the state's land is in agricultural production, substantially more than in any

other New England state. And while in 1983 the farm industry itself contributed only 5 percent of the state's gross product, the aesthetic value of Vermont's pastoral landscape is far greater. The bucolic scenes—open meadows, plowed fields, cows and barns—along the state's highways give Vermont its particular appeal and help make tourism one of the leading "industries." It now accounts for 15 percent of the state's income. As one resident put it, "When travelling in Vermont, one feels the landscape is open and airy. In contrast, driving across New Hampshire, which has many fewer working farms, is like moving through a tunnel of trees. When people come to our state, they just expect to see farms—like they expect to see orange groves in Florida, white sand beaches and palm trees. But even more than this, farms are not just our popular image, they are the soul of Vermont's character."

While these utopian visions of Vermont once were not so far from actuality, they are increasingly mere hopeful fantasies about a place that has come to share the prosperity, and problems, of the rest of the nation. Suburbia is a way of life, if not yet a predominant landscape feature, for much of the state's populace. The small communities are robbed of their social and politi-

PHYSIOGRAPHIC AREAS

Vermont has five distinct physiographic areas: the Lake Champlain Lowlands, the Taconic Mountains, the Valley of Vermont, the Vermont Piedmont and the Northeast Highlands.

The Lake Champlain Lowland overlaps with a geographic region of the same name, but usually is defined more by its social and political personality than by the physiographic area proper. The Lowland is part of a structural trough that was created in a massive slippage of the earth's crust. The valley is about 20 miles wide and dominated by Lake Champlain, the sixth-largest freshwater lake in the nation. A highly significant resource, the lake recently was nominated for International Biosphere Preserve status. It forms a scenic backdrop for Vermont's largest city of Burlington and moderates the local climate, giving this area one of the longest growing seasons in the state. Flat and fertile, the Lowland is the state's agricultural heart and is typified by the broad squares of cultivated fields, dotted at the margins by operating farms.

Eighty-five percent of the state is classified as hilly or mountainous. The major upland feature is the Green Mountain range, which consists of several parallel ridges running north and south the length of the state. A number of these ridges have individual names such as the Northfield Mountains, Worcester Mountains, Lowell Mountains and Sterling Range, but really are nothing more than subsidiaries of the main mountain chain.

The Green Mountains, in turn, are a northern extension of the Appalachians, and have 80 peaks rising more than 3,000' above sea level, seven that top 4,000'. They posed a serious obstacle to the first settlers.

For early travelers few routes crossed the range. The easiest travelways were along the rivers like the Winooski and the Lamoille, that cut entirely through the mountains from east to west. Called antecedent streams by geologists, these rivers existed before the uplift of the Green Mountains. As the land rose, the water continued to cut downwards, eventually forming impressive watergaps that even today are important natural corridors. Paralleling the Winooski, for example, is Interstate 89.

Although cleared pastures once crowded even the summits of these mountains, today most of the range is reforested and is either part of the Green Mountain National Forest or under state ownership. The Green Mountains serve as a major recreation area and most of Vermont's ski resorts sit along its spine. Because of its overall high elevation, few large communities inhabit the mountains, and several such as Glastenbury in the southern end of the state, are now ghost towns.

The Taconic Mountains straddle the Vermont-New York border and tend to be more rugged, though slightly lower in elevation, than the Green Mountain range. Mt. Equinox at 3,816' is the highest Taconic peak. The Taconics once were deforested for agriculture, but today, for the most part, the slopes have reverted to woodlands. Slate and marble quarrying were important here and, although the industry has survived to the present, fewer companies are in business. today

Lying between the Green and Taconic Mountains is the relatively flat, 85-mile-long Valley of Vermont. Eight to 10 miles wide near Bennington, it narrows to a few hundred yards near Emerald Lake. The valley has served as a travel corridor since the time of the Indians, and today U.S. Highway 7 follows the route of ancient trails. A major divide near the midpoint of the valley sheds waters to the Hudson River via the Battenkill drainage and those eventually reaching the St. Lawrence by way of Otter Creek and Lake Champlain.

East of the Green Mountains, an area of rolling, hilly

The view south from Mt. Mansfield, Vermont's highest summit, in the Green Mountains. GEORGE WUERTHNER

country is known to geographers as the Vermont Piedmont, which means literally "foot-mountain." Numerous, ancient intrusions of molten magma formed the ore pockets that sustained the area's quarries and mines. Rising above the

general level of the hilly terrain are isolated mountains called monadnocks. Burke Mountain and Mt. Ascutney are two such peaks resulting from the erosion of softer rock around the more resistant granite intrusions. The Connecticut River

borders this area and the east side of the state.

Lying in the extreme northeast corner of the state is the Northeast Highland. It covers most of the social/cultural region known as the Northeast Kingdom. Underlain by granite, with poor drainage

and undulating topography, this area is infested with mosquitoes and black flies in summer and gripped by frigid winter temperatures. This part of Vermont was the last to be settled and the first to be abandoned. It is Vermont's least-populated area.

Tourism is now the state's second largest industry and accounts for 15 percent of Vermont's annual gross income. JOHN LYNCH

cal significance as people view the larger towns and cities more and more as economic and social centers. When neighbors no longer meet on Main Street, exchange news and salutations after the Sunday morning service, or in other ways participate in the everyday affairs of their village or town, it is difficult to maintain a strong sense of community loyalty and responsibility.

Other institutions are strained as well. The stronghold of true democracy, the Vermont Town Meeting, seems to function adequately in matters of town highway maintenance and how much to pay municipal employees, but it cannot properly address larger, more complex issues like urban sprawl, resort development or solid-waste disposal. And many of Vermont's farmers, once the paradigms of self-sufficiency, would be out of business without government price supports, special buy-outs and other programs that make them anything but independent yeomen.

The truth is that in Vermont, as elsewhere, the family farm is rapidly becoming a thing of the past, and most Vermonters today work in manufacturing. In 1982 manufacturing accounted for 27 percent of the gross state product and the largest employers are the electronics and high technology industries. Many factors account for the strong growth of this industry in the state, in general best described as "quality of life." To an ever-increasing number of people, Vermont seems to possess an enviable balance between development and environmental protection, between natural and country-side landscapes and city amenities.

The influx of new residents has changed the Vermont social fabric and widened the rift between the poor and the privileged. While many new jobs were created in the 1970s and 1980s, most have gone to well educated newcomers— many of them refugees from megalopolis. And while we picture the classic Vermont home as a white colonial clapboard on the village green, a great number of natives dwell in decrepit shacks or ramshackle trailers, tucked in some dark hollow. Long-time Vermonters, and their sons and daughters, are finding it increasingly difficult to get by in their native state, in spite of the new prosperity. Land and housing are increasingly priced out of the reach of the average blue-collar worker, and are bought instead by the new immigrants with the jobs and salaries to finance higher standards of living.

The backwoods inhabitants, these poorer natives, are sometimes derisively referred to as "woodchucks" by the less indigent. They are often the descendants of hill farmers who gave up trying to coax a living from the miserly earth and went to work instead on the highway crews, in the mills and for construction companies. Mobile homes are often the only housing they can afford, big pick-ups are their favored means of transportation. One patriotic fellow eyeing a Toyota stated: "Only Fords or Chevy's. We only drive American-made trucks around here."

The backwoods Vermonter uses his non-import vehicle to haul firewood, which keeps him warm during the long, cold winters. He burns wood because it's cheap, not because he thinks it's ethically correct or aesthetically appealing. After working hard all week at some physically demanding job like construction, he's not likely to put on a pair of cross-country skis and struggle up a hillside. Instead he opts for a snowmobile and brisk ride over old logging roads and fields.

The opening day of deer season is a serious holiday, and every year the debate over doe hunting rages while the sportsmen recuperate in the evenings in the local tavern. The second most important annual ritual takes place on the first day of the fishing season in April when these Vermont-born residents don their plaid shirts, grab their bait and bobber, and head for the nearest lake. While most Vermont backwoodsmen love and appreciate the beauty of their native state, many make it clear they can't live on "scenic income" alone; they are usually supportive of any development that promises more and better-paying jobs. As one plaid-shirted logger said, "You can't eat blue sky."

The newcomers, derisively called flatlanders by the natives, now comprise some 40 percent of the state's population. Born and raised out-of-state, often in urban or suburban areas, these immigrants tend to be wealthier, better educated and more liberal than their Vermont-born counterparts. To the new Vermonters, their adopted state promises the fulfillment of a dream—living the simple, good life in a country setting. But these newcomers do not abandon all the amenities of civilization when they move here. They set their compact disc stereos on the old barn-board bookshelf; drive Saab Turbos down the washboarded dirt road; frequent the chic eateries that have multiplied since their arrival.

New residents often move into a renovated farmhouse or purchase a five-acre parcel in the country, and then tack up "No hunting or trespassing" signs around their property. Nothing raises a native's hackles higher than encountering posted land in a place where he has hunted for years. Unfortunately, the newcomers are often merely ignorant of, not antagonistic to, the Vermont tradition of allowing public access to one's private lands.

There are other differences. Coming from a depersonalized urban background, a new Vermonter is less likely to see the local community as a vehicle for solving social and political questions. Although he may staunchly defend the town meeting for its symbolic value, he looks instead toward the state or federal government to address such issues as environmental degradation, or the loss of open farmland. It is largely these politically active newcomers who broke the Republican party's long hold on the state and brought about the recent elections of Democrat and independent candidates.

While they may work during the week inside an office, many newcomers like to spend their free time outdoors, engaged in some physical activity like downhill skiing or backpacking. These ex-urbanites usually don't hunt, but many enjoy fishing like their native-born neighbors. The only difference is that the recent Vermonters are usually fly fishermen; the old-time residents are bait fishermen.

Above: End of a winter day in Manchester. Neat villages are as much a part of Vermont's appeal as its farm landscapes.
Left: Wood heat is a way of life for rural Vermonters and an economical way of getting through the cold Vermont winter. Barney Bruns of Roxbury carries a load of split wood from his shed.
GEORGE WUERTHNER PHOTOS

Above: Despite Vermont's early dependency on agriculture, manufacturing has always played an important role in its economy. Today manufacturing leads all other economic activities in the state.
VERMONT HISTORICAL SOCIETY

Right: Old farmhouse near Shaftsbury reflects the care and tidiness that make Vermont such an attractive place for resident and visitor.
GEORGE WUERTHNER

Because they came here for the charm of Vermont's villages and the wholesomeness of the unindustrialized environment, a large portion of the recent immigrants strongly support zoning regulations and land-use planning to limit development and seek to maintain the rural nature of the state. They vigorously oppose new growth in the state, often, say natives, after they have already purchased their own little 10-acre mini-farm in the country. It's what one old-time Vermonter cynically described as the "once in, lock the door syndrome."

Natives and Newcomers

Each group— newcomers and native-born residents— has different ideas about what Vermont should be and how best to achieve it. One of the clearest examples of these divergent viewpoints could be heard at a 1987 town meeting. The debate centered on whether a particular stretch of dirt road should be paved. The relatively recent residents of the town expressed their desire to keep the road as it was. They worried that traffic and development would increase if the road were blacktopped. Several said the dirt road was charming— a part of old Vermont they loved. This last comment left one old timer truly flabbergasted, and he retorted that he failed to see anything charming about dusty roads or having to pull his vehicles out of the bottomless quagmires that appeared every mud season at the end of winter. He'd had enough charm to last his lifetime— he wanted the road paved. Finally, a compromise was reached; the road would be improved, but left unpaved.

Natives and newcomers seem to lack at times an appreciation for what the other group represents and provides for all Vermonters. Newcomers may wax eloquent about the Vermont character, portrayed in stories and Rockwell-esque paintings, but simultaneously condemn the local woodchucks who are, after all, the descendants of those sturdy Yankee farmers so celebrated in the state's mythology. And while many old Vermonters speak contemptuously of flatlanders, it is the influx of new people that has brought about the state's economic renaissance. For generations, Vermont was a land of very limited opportunity, making it "a good place to be from" but not a place to stay. Today, native youth can more readily find employment in the state.

Despite the class distinctions that operate— mostly below the surface— in Vermont society, there are few racial differences. Most native Vermonters are descended from old New England Yankees; the first settlers were originally colonists of Connecticut, Massachusetts and Rhode Island. The few foreign-born immigrants came to the state in the late 1800s. Skilled stone cutters from Italy, Scotland and Wales were recruited to work in the quarries, and Irishmen helped to build the railroads. The various ethnic groups were assimilated into the general social fabric within one generation, and in all but their last names, these Vermonters are nearly indistinguishable from the sons and daughters of slightly earlier pioneers.

There is one immigrant group, however, that has remained somewhat separate from the mainstream of Vermont society. These people came not from Europe, but from Canada. They are the French-Canadians, and in northern Vermont they constitute a significant segment of the population. In 1980, 37 percent of the state's residents claimed French heritage. One can observe their influence when driving northwards through the state, as the Protestant churches in the southern region give way to Catholic churches in the northern shires, and as one spots here and there a highway sign in both French and English. The French-Canadians first came to work in the mills by Burlington, in the logging camps of the Northeast Kingdom and to farm in the Champlain Lowlands. For the most part, their descendants still call Vermont home, but because of their language differences and traditions they have remained somewhat outside of the mainstream social fabric and as such have reaped fewer of the benefits that other immigrant groups have enjoyed once they were assimilated into the Vermont Yankee cultural tradition.

The relative dearth of racial and cultural diversity can be attributed to Vermont's long residence on the back road of America—a place no one was striving to reach and a place many had to leave. Of New England states, Vermont was settled late. Uncertainty about the validity of land grants, the rugged nature of the terrain and the scarcity of good farm land, threats of attack from Indians, the French and later the British, and Vermont's insecure status as an independent republic for 14 years, all served to delay colonization by whites.

As lands opened farther west in the Ohio Valley and Midwest, many Vermonters packed up and moved on. By 1850, 43 percent of the state's native-born were living outside its borders and many of the hill farms they had started were abandoned and reverting to trees. Ten years later the state's growth had slowed considerably; the population stood at 315,089 and would remain nearly static for a hundred years. The 1960 census showed only 389,881 residents. For decades, two out of every five Vermonters left the state to seek opportunities elsewhere.

In the 1960s the trend was reversed and more people began to move to the state than left it. Between 1960 and 1980 the state's population rose by 121,000 people and by the last year, more than 40 percent of the population had been born and raised outside of the state. Part of this growth can be attributed to better transportation, including the construction of an interstate highway system that made travel from metropolitan regions like Boston, Montreal and New York easy, safe, comfortable and quick. Vermont has 320 miles of interstate and no town is more than 45 miles from one of these major arteries. Rapid and dependable transportation also spawned the growth of new light industries, such as the manufacture of computer and electronics parts, that did not require a local market and could be shipped inexpensively throughout the world.

Recreation Paradise

One reason businesses began to seek a Vermont location was its reputation as a recreation paradise. From sailing on Lake Champlain to skiing at Stowe, Vermont seems to have it all. Also, strong government commit-

Many Vermonters are independent craftsmen and 10 percent of the state's residents are self-employed. Vermont is second only to agricultural Montana for having a high proportion of self-employment.
STEVE KAUFMAN

Agriculture falls well behind manufacturing and tourism in contribution to the state's gross economic income, but it contributes much to the Vermont mythology and thus plays an important role in the state's attractiveness for tourism and the location of new industry.
STEVE KAUFMAN

ments to a clean environment and quality public education contributed to the state's increasing popularity as a desirable place to live.

The advent of fast travel systems also has transformed the state's tourist industry, which is now second-largest employer in the state. New York, Boston, Cleveland, Washington, Ottawa, Toronto, Montreal, Pittsburgh and Philadelphia are all within 500 miles of the state—a one-day drive on the interstate system. While Vermont has been a popular haven for the upper class since the 19th century, tourism's real blossoming arrived in the middle of this century, when Americans as a whole were beginning to enjoy greater mobility and prosperity. Summer was the main vacation season, bringing multitudes of sightseers—many of whom fell in love with the lush Green Mountains and bought farms or lake frontage where they could have their holiday retreat. Some of these summer-home areas have acquired a reputation for a specific clientele. For example, Caspian Lake near Greensboro is known as the summer sanctuary of college professors and literati from the Northeast.

Until the development of downhill skiing as a viable, popular sport, Vermont's visitors came almost entirely in the warm weather months and during the fall foliage season. Many resort areas became virtual ghost towns during the long winters. In the 1930s the first rope tow was built on a hill near Woodstock. By the start of World War II, there were tows and ski trails at Stowe, East Corinth, Brattleboro, Pico Peak and Bromley Mountain. With the general prosperity that followed the war, Vermont's ski industry continued to expand, so that by the 1983-84 season it was contributing $230 million directly to the state economy. Yet surprisingly few ski areas actually consistently turn a profit from their operations and, contrary to popular thought, the number of areas has declined in recent years, from 81 in 1970 to 47 by 1987.

Only three other state economies depend more on tourism than Vermont, and the industry is being called upon increasingly to fill the void left by other, fading businesses. In 1980, for example, there were 2,650 jobs in the furniture industry, but by 1984 there were only 1,800. Seven hundred people worked in the state's quarries in 1980, but by 1984 this had declined to 500 employees. In contrast, tourism continues to offer more jobs every year. The Killington ski area employs 1,800 people during the peak of their winter season.

The greatest number of visitors still come to the state in the summer— 7 million at last count— but the autumn foliage season is a much more hectic time, as some 1 million leaf peepers jam the roadways in a brief three-week period. By comparison, the skiing business attracts 1.5 million people during its six-month-long season.

The abundance of tourist-trade jobs and profits does have its price. Many once-peaceful rural towns have been transformed almost overnight into trendy vacation destinations, making them too expensive for many Vermonters to remain. As one Forest Service employee working in Manchester said, "For those of us on more or less fixed incomes, it's difficult to survive in these resort towns. I live in Arlington and commute because I can't afford to live in Manchester anymore. It's just too expensive."

The subdivision of rural real estate and construction of condominiums occurs throughout the state, but is especially intense in or near ski resorts. Most of these developments are built in smaller towns, where the existing infrastructure of roads, sewer and water systems, and other town services like police protection, is not equal to the sudden surge in population. The environmental repercussions can be great as well; water quality, wildlife habitat, and scenic mountain slopes and open land may all be endangered by careless development. These threats to Vermont's high-quality environment, both human and natural, prompted in 1970 the passage of landmark legislation— a law known today as Act 250— which regulates land-use change through a process of development applications and review. Act 250 enables state officials to assess the potential impacts of proposed projects, whereupon they may require mitigatory measures or even completely reject an application.

Most new subdivisions, recreational homesites and condominiums are sold to out-of-state owners. By 1980 more than half of the private property in Vermont was owned by non-Vermonters or corporations based outside the state borders. The trend toward increasing out-of-state ownership and control is reflected by industry, where every large company operating in the state, including the traditional businesses like rock quarrying, is owned by non-residents. More and more, Vermonters feel that outsiders are calling the shots, and in a sense they are right. Nonetheless, Vermont has undeniably become a very good place to be, with an unemployment rate of 3.7 percent in 1987— one of the lowest in the nation— and an ever-expanding range of educational, cultural and recreational opportunities.

Over its 300-year written history, Vermont developed as it did largely as a result of the nature of its physical land base. The physiographic setting dictated where people first settled, the routes they took within and beyond the state, where and what industries developed, even the character of Vermonters themselves. Early manufacturing centers like Springfield were located on waterfalls, which provided power. Burlington became an early shipping and lumber center, situated as it is on Lake Champlain and once surrounded by vast pine forests. Today the mountains are a valuable resource for the ski and the tourist industry in general.

Except for the Lake Champlain Lowlands, Vermont lacks substantial tracts of flat, fertile ground, which is the major reason it saw little development for nearly a century following its initial settlement. Historians have speculated that if the rich farmlands to the west had been available slightly earlier to migrant pioneers, Vermont would have remained a virtually uninhabited wilderness. Thus the land shaped the state's political and social history, too, making it a stable but conservative fiefdom, where few new residents and few new ideas disrupted the even flow of events.

As Vermont's economy takes advantage of tourism and the waves of high-tech growth spreading from eastern cities, young Vermonters have a chance to think about building a future at home, instead of looking outward for employment.
TED LEVIN

Vermont is now in transition from being a rural backwater to taking its place as an active participant in the modern, high-tech world. While the state aggressively recruits new businesses and industry and develops world-class resorts, Vermonters must reconcile future economic growth and opportunity with their wish to maintain the best of the present and the past. They must find ways to keep the desirable aspects of the Vermont mythology alive.

Will Vermont's growth and development mean the loss of its unique character— its pastoral landscapes, its meticulous, proud people? Progressive laws such as Act 250, and residents' faith in the special qualities that make Vermont worth calling home— including strong communities and a tradition of respect for divergent opinions— are the ultimate promise of bright tomorrows. Then, Vermonters hope, their state will be not only a good place to be from, but the ideal place to remain.

CHAPTER TWO

GEOLOGICAL SETTING

The rocks on Isle La Motte, at the northern end of Lake Champlain, bear the remains of an ancient coral reef. Corals inhabit very warm, tropical seas, so such fossils occurring on an island surrounded by cold fresh-water are somewhat puzzling. We know the basin now filled by Lake Champlain once was covered by a shallow sea because of the telltale limestone bedrock, which could only have developed in a marine environment. But tropical Vermont? This seems even more difficult to imagine than the Green Mountain State's once having a seacoast.

Geologists believe that the landmass now comprising Vermont was at one time in its distant past actually nearer the equator. More precisely, the rock of Isle La Motte was formed in a tropical region of the globe, and subsequently moved to its present location. The migration of the fossil-bearing rock, as well as that of entire continents, is explained by the theory of plate tectonics.

The earth's crust is made up of large plates that float on a layer of semi-solid rock called the mantle. Radioactive decay occurring deep in the earth creates great amounts of heat, melting the interior rocks, setting up convection currents that circulate molten rock beneath the earth's crust and rafting the plates that make up the world's continents like ice pans in a river. They jostle against each other; some may break apart. In the course of all this shuffling over geologic time, the size, shape and number, as well as location, of the plates has changed. Thus, a bit of 500-million-year old coral in the northern corner of Vermont.

Plate tectonics explains more than the past movement of continental rocks; it provides a clue to present geological processes. The rocks that make up continents tend to be granitic and lighter than the basalts that dominate ocean basins. When an oceanic plate collides with a continental one, a period of mountain building ensues as the force of impact causes the continental plate edges to buckle upward. The oceanic plate, meanwhile, is shoved downwards into the earth's mantle. Deep trenches form where this occurs. Volcanoes are commonly associated with these collisions, as we see today in the Cascades of Washington and Oregon, where the Pacific plate is diving under the now-westward-moving North American plate.

The grinding together of these giant masses produces molten magma. When the magma rises but fails to reach the surface, it cools slowly in place, creating a hard durable rock known as granite. At the trailing end of a colliding continental plate is bedrock undergoing erosion and weathering. The eastern edge of North America is just such a "back fender," riding on the westward-moving plate. Here, mountains gradually are broken down into sediments and swept by water and wind back to the sea.

Shaping the Mountains

All the processes described above were involved in the shaping of Vermont's mountains, which are a northern extension of the Appalachian Range. What are now called the Green Mountains and Taconic Mountains had their ancestral beginnings more than a billion years ago when several continental plates collided and produced an early precursor of the Appalachian Range. Most of this ancient rock was worn away by subsequent erosion or buried under younger deposits, but outcroppings can be seen on Killington and Pico peaks in the Green Mountains.

About 500 million years ago, the North American plate began slowly to grind its way toward Europe. It

The folded layers originally deposited as sediments in an ancient sea have been folded and warped by pressure and heat into the metamorphic rock seen here in the Green Mountains. ROBERT PERRON

Facing page: The Green Mountains as well as other highlands in the state are the exposed roots of once much higher mountain ranges, which have been exposed by the relentless erosion of water carried by such streams as the Roaring Branch, seen here near Kelly Stand.
GEORGE WUERTHNER

overrode an ancient ocean basin that was forced beneath its advancing edge. Like the process occurring today on the West Coast, the friction between the sideswiping plates resulted in volcanic activity as molten rock, or magma, rose to the surface and erupted.

In addition, the land at the leading edge of the North American plate was crumpled upwards, creating the Appalachian Mountain chain. This succession of parallel ridges runs generally north and south, from the Gaspé Peninsula in Canada to Alabama. In the process of uplift the sedimentary rocks that had been deposited in shallow basins along the continent's edge were folded, squeezed and deformed. The heat and pressure transformed the sedimentary material into a different, metamorphic rock. The slate, marble, gneiss and schist that make up much of the Green and Taconic mountains are examples of these altered materials. Along the western edge of the state can be found some unchanged sedimentary rocks that escaped the metamorphic processes. These include a belt of limestone that runs along the edge of Lake Champlain and through Isle La Motte.

Granite is the basement rock that underlies nearly all continental masses. It is formed by the slow cooling of magma beneath the earth's outer crust. Occasionally, through a combination of uplift and erosion, granitic intrusions are exposed to the surface. Outcrops can be found in the Green Mountains and the Northeast Kingdom, and dotting the Vermont Piedmont on the east side of the state.

Many of these granitic intrusions are considerably younger in age than the surrounding bedrock. For instance, the granite laid bare on Mt. Ascutney was formed approximately 122 million years ago (similar in age to New Hampshire's White Mountains) and is some of the youngest exposed rock in the state. Because granite is extremely hard and resists erosion, many of these granitic intrusions remain as isolated peaks, or monadnocks.

The circulation of fiery-hot magma often precipitates minerals from surrounding bedrock. When these super-heated "juices" cool, they leave the normally-scarce elements in concentrated veins or ore bodies. Gold often is found in lodes along the fringes of magma intrusions, and although gold mining is most often associated with the West, gold has been discovered in a number of Vermont locations. Many small gold mines dot the hills near Bridgewater Corners west of Woodstock, and placer gold still can be sluiced from gravels in Broad Brook and the Ottauquechee River near Plymouth. But before you sell the house and head for the hills, take note: In today's economy, there's probably a whole lot more profit in the Vermont winters' "white gold," and the golden colors of autumn than in the sparse flakes you're apt to find in the Green Mountains.

In addition to the extraction of gold, silver and lead, the most significant— and profitable— mining was for the copper bodies at Strafford, Corinth and Richford. Vermont once was a leading copper producer, rivaling the deposits of Michigan's Upper Peninsula and of Butte, Montana.

Although Vermont has never yielded truly large quantities of metallic minerals, it is well known for its production of talc, slate, marble and granite. These, and other minerals, form the bedrock of the state's two major mountain ranges, The Taconic range long puzzled geologists because its bedrock, primarily slates and shales, is of a type also found to the east, on the other side of the Green Mountains, but did not seem to logically relate to the rocks immediately adjacent to it. Scientists speculate that in the geologic event that gave birth to the Appalachian Mountains, these ancient sedimentary rocks were uplifted, then shoved westward onto the slowly rising rocks of the Green Mountains. The further hoisting of the Green Mountains tipped the overlying shales westward, whereupon they slid off into their present-day location. The tremendous pressure and heat involved in such gargantuan movements caused the metamorphosis of many of the sedimentary strata, changing limestones and shales to marbles and slates for which the state is renowned.

Plate movements also have resulted in the development of major faults, or regions where the earth's crust has been broken and pulled apart. The Lone Rock fault can be seen along Lake Champlain just north of Burlington. Here, older white dolomite is clearly seen overlying the younger black shale. This "overthrust fault" formed some 200 million years ago when one crustal block overrode an adjacent fragment. In other parts of the world these particular geologic formations have been found to harbor large deposits of oil and gas. Thus, the "Eastern Overthrust Belt" has recently been the object of much interest and exploration. Although natural gas has been found, the great depth of the deposits precludes development at this time.

Plate tectonics set the boundaries of Vermont's landscape and built the basic structure upon which its present scenery rests, but it was the forces of glaciation that reworked the surface features and gave the state its distinctive appearance. For reasons still not fully understood, the earth's average temperature periodically drops and snowfall increases around the globe. After successive years of increased snow accumulation, in which more snow falls than melts, the weight of the built-up layers compacts the once light and fluffy material into glacial ice. Eventually large areas of the northern and southern hemispheres become covered with the glaciers.

An Age of Glaciers

Over a great span of time, the glaciers grow so large they begin to create their own weather. This occurs due to a phenomenon known as orographic uplift. At its height, the glacial ice that covered North America was more than 10,000' thick. This is more than twice the height of the highest Vermont mountain and, as any hiker knows, the higher one climbs, the cooler it usually gets. As the continental glaciers slowly ground their way south, they created a moving "mountain front" that forced air masses to rise, cool and precipitate their moisture, above the glacial ice. The precipitation usually was snow, and contributed to the height and size of these great ice mountains. During the last glacial period, so

much of the world's water was bound up as ice that the oceans were more than 475' lower than today!

Difficult as it may be to comprehend, glacial ice actually flows, although we normally think of ice as brittle and hard. The bottom of a glacier is under a tremendous pressure from the weight of the layers above it, and it behaves like a soft plastic or cold honey, oozing ever so slowly along the path of least resistance—usually down a valley rather than up and over a hill. The continental glaciers that moved south from Canada were so large, however, they had the power to ride over hills and mountains, burying everything in their path. The grinding ice reshaped the Vermont landscape, leaving many reminders of its passage, including U-shaped valleys, kame terraces, moraines, eskers, erratics, cirques and glacially-polished rocks.

One of the most common indicators of past glaciation is the exposed and smoothed bedrock found throughout the state. Boulders and rocks frozen in the glacier, under the weight of tons of ice, acted like giant files, rasping and scraping at the higher knobs and points and smoothing them. The low spots were filled with excess rock. Fine scratches on bedrock surfaces, called striations, are usually seen aligned north-to-south, indicating the direction in which the ice was moving.

All of Vermont's higher peaks were rounded by the Ice Age glaciers; this is one reason for their overall gentle appearance. Ice filled existing valleys and sheared off rocky prominences, steepened valley walls and flattened the bottoms by covering them with glacial till. A classic U-shaped profile was the result, such as that of the trough containing Lake Willoughby.

Smaller tributary glaciers sometimes formed on the slopes of high peaks and carved out amphitheater-like basins called cirques. Tuckerman's Ravine in New Hampshire's White Mountains is a cirque and many peaks in the New York State Adirondacks also bear these glacially-scooped features on their flanks. There is nothing in Vermont that unquestionably can be termed a cirque, though there are a few likely candidates, such as the Miller Brook "cirque" south of Mt. Mansfield.

The ice at the base of a glacier remains somewhat plastic under pressure, but if the weight above is removed—as when the glacier passes over a peak and drops off the opposite side of the summit in a sort of slow-motion "waterfall"—the basal ice may solidify momentarily to bedrock. Then as the ice advances farther, it pulls the rocks loose creating a jagged, broken slope.

The distinctive steep southern slope of Camel's Hump illustrates the powerful plucking action of glacial ice.

The advancing glacial front emulates a sluggish bulldozer, pushing debris into piles of unsorted rock, gravel and boulders called moraines. A glacier is also like a conveyor belt that carries material it picks up along the way, to eventually dump it at its terminus, or snout. If a glacier remains relatively stationary, neither advancing nor retreating, it will continue to unload huge amounts of moraine at one spot. When the glacier retreats, it leaves behind these rocky deposits in the form of long low hills, such as those making up Long Island and Cape Cod. Giant moraines like that are absent from Vermont, but low hills of glacial origin do grace the landscape. Newport, on the south end of Lake Memphremagog, is built partially on a moraine. Other moraines can be seen south of Rutland, near St. Johnsbury and in northeast Vermont.

After the Glaciers

When a glacier retreats rapidly, as did the ice over much of Vermont, the moraine material is spread out evenly over the land as glacial till. It is this unsorted, rocky covering that characterizes much of Vermont's landscape and even determined its history to a great extent. The state's relatively late settlement and subsequent farmland abandonment during the 1800s partially can be attributed to its glacial heritage. As the original settlers soon discovered, the passage of the glaciers left Vermont with a good stock of boulders and stones and a short supply of topsoil. Before they could farm the land, these pioneering Vermonters had to laboriously carry the assorted rocks and boulders to the edges of their fields. Each winter and spring, the frost would heave up new rocks and the process was repeated. In an act of Yankee thrift, farmers constructed stone fences out of the rubble they collected. Today these walls are a distinctive feature of the New England landscape— a legacy of the Ice Age and the tenacity of Vermont's farmers.

Another glacial deposit for which humans have found even greater utility is the kame terrace. These sand and gravel remnants are common in most Vermont valleys, and developed when the glaciers began to melt and retreat northward. The ice disappeared first from the mountaintops while thick lobes lingered in the valleys. Meltwater streams, carrying very heavy sediment loads, washed off the mountains and onto the ice below. The sands, gravels and small stones were spewed out as deltas or outwash plains. Eventually the ice melted completely and these stream-sorted deposits were left in

place along the margins of the valley. Today they are extensively used as gravel pits.

Occasionally one comes upon a rock resting in the midst of a pasture or on top of smooth, solid bedrock. Like ships sitting on dry land, they seem strange and out of place. Appropriately, such rocks are called erratics and were plucked by a glacier from their original mountainside location, to be set down seemingly at whim. Erratics are a fairly common feature of the Vermont countryside and even crown the summit of Mt. Mans-

Birches line the shore of Lake Champlain. Lake Champlain occupies a structural trough or break in the earth's crust, which later was scoured deeper by the passage of glaciers.

Facing page: Glaciers delivered the large rocks that dot many Vermont pastures, like these near Granby.
GEORGE WUERTHNER PHOTOS

field, providing evidence that glaciers once completely covered Vermont's highest peak.

The glaciers also had much to do with the making of Vermont's lakes. A look at any good state map shows that nearly all of Vermont's lakes are narrow and long, like fingers, and are generally oriented in a north-south direction. The Finger Lakes of New York are particularly spectacular examples of glacially-carved waterbodies, but Vermont has a few, more modest specimens of its own. Lake Willoughby in the Northeast Kingdom is the state's best known "finger" lake. It was formed after a glacier ground through an existing river valley, deepening the basin and oversteepening the sides to create the spectacular cliffs on Mt. Pisgah and Mt. Hor. Moraine and till deposited at either end of the valley dammed water in the basin and Lake Willoughby was born. Other lakes such as St. Catherine, Bomoseen, Crystal, Groton, Carmi, Maidstone, Seymour, Gillett Pond and Great Averill Pond owe at least part of their origins to glacial action.

Vermont's most spectacular lake is also an Ice Age artifact. The Champlain basin, a trench born millions of years ago in a major fault movement between the Adirondack and Green mountains, was a natural glacier pathway during the last Ice Age. The ice dug the basin, and when the glacier retreated to the north, the ice blocked the northward-flowing meltwaters. The resulting Glacial Lake Vermont eventually reached a depth of perhaps 1,200'. At its maximum, lake waters lapped against the Green Mountains and covered the present sites of towns like Middlebury, Brandon, Burlington and Addison under hundreds of feet of water. The ancient shorelines are still visible on hills throughout the Lake Champlain lowlands. Unlike the modern lake which empties into Canadian waters, the glacial lake was forced by the icy barrier at its northern end to drain southward. Glacial Lake Vermont flowed into the Hudson River through a gorge it carved near present-day Coveville, New York.

There were other glacial lakes in Vermont; at one time they covered nearly half the state. For instance, waters backed up from an ice dam on the Hudson River covered portions of the towns of Bennington, Arlington and Pownal in the southwest corner of the state. A number of glacial lakes, collectively called Lake Hitchcock, were formed in the Connecticut River valley. The rivers feeding all these Ice Age waterbodies carried heavy loads of fine silt that gradually settled out in the lakes' still waters. Today, the resulting soils are rich and stone-free— the prime agricultural lands of the state.

Quechee Gorge, Vermont's deepest canyon, was carved by the erosive power of running water. JEFF GNASS

QUARRIES

When you take an antacid, you might well be consuming a tiny bit of Vermont. Use of Vermont's limestone as filler in pharmaceutical products is merely one new application of an old Vermont product— its quarry rocks. Since 1761 when the French took Chazy limestone out of Isle La Motte, the sale of stone has been big business. Slate, granite, talc, asbestos and marble all at one time or another were cut from the state's mountains and shipped throughout the world.

Marble was one of Vermont's first major commodities. Excluding the Chazy limestone on Isle La Motte, which is limestone labelled black marble, the first marble to be quarried in the state was at Dorset and Pittsford in 1785. These two locations are still the main centers of Vermont's marble industry, which runs in a belt from Manchester north to Shelburne.

Technically, marble is a form of sedimentary limestone that has been metamorphosed into a crystalline mineral known as calcite or dolomite. Other rocks are called, and sold commercially as, marble—although they are not such to geologists. These include the Chazy limestone found on Lake Champlain's islands; Champlain marble, a slightly metamorphosed sandstone quarried just east of the Chazy limestone in a belt from Mallets Head near Burlington, north nearly to Swanton; and serpentine rocks marketed as Verde Antique marble, which were taken from a north-south belt following the east flank of the Green Mountains from Rochester to Roxbury. The serpentines have absolutely no geologic or chemical relationship to marble, but apparently that fact was no bar to tagging it as such.

Early marble quarries were the major suppliers of gravestones. Indeed, one way to gauge the approximate age of a cemetery is to measure the relative proportion of marble monuments to the later granite stones. The latter rock did not begin to replace marble until the 1900s. Some marble was exported for building stone, but the high transportation costs prohibited the expansion of this market. From 1860 and on, however, the railroads provided relatively inexpensive means of transporting the heavy stone, and the industry boomed. From 1880 to 1930, Vermont was the leading producer of marble in the United States. Today the demand for cut marble has declined, although the state remains at the forefront in the production of dimension, or building, marble.

While cut and polished marble is no longer a major product, the stone industry has expanded into other lines. Fine-textured, ground limestone has many wide uses as a filler agent, in pharmaceutical products, in tires, chewing gum, plastics, caulking materials

and floor tiles. Limestone is also chopped and ground to make lime for agriculture and filler for road construction.

A second early quarry industry centered around the production of slate. Slate is metamorphosed shale, and ranges in color from red to blue and black. It was used for a variety of things, including blackboards, school slates, gravestones, pool table tops and roofing tiles. Many an old barn and house in Vermont is roofed with the durable, thin slate tiles that largely have been replaced these days by cheaper asphalt roofing. Today slate furnishes colorful flagstone for patios and walkways, or

is crushed and used in tennis court surfacing.

Although slate is found in several areas in Vermont, the largest and most important belt exists along the New York-Vermont border in the Taconic Mountains. The industry is centered in the towns of Sudbury, Hubbardton, Castleton, Poultney and West Pawlet. The earliest slate diggings began in 1839 when the rock was used locally for roofing tile, but with the arrival of the railroads, expansion into national markets was possible.

The last major quarry stone, and most economically important, is granite. One of

the first uses for Vermont granite was in the building of the state capitol in Montpelier. The edifice was completed in 1838. Although granite was a popular construction material, as with other dimension stone, it took the coming of the railroads in 1888 to make the quarry operation at Barre a national granite producer. By 1914, granite surpassed marble to become Vermont's leading stone export. Nearly 75 percent was for gravestones and monuments—a market, one might say, with long-term promise.

Vermont's quarries once held a prominent spot in the state's employment picture, but by 1985 only 485 workers listed mining and quarrying as their occupation. Some, however, had branched into other related areas of employment such as stone shaping and polishing. In the Barre area alone, 60 businesses employ nearly 1,500 workers in industries related to rock quarrying.

Left: Vermont's quarries were responsible for the immigration of stone cutters from Italy, Scotland and Wales.
Top: Blanchard granite quarry near Barre in 1895. By 1985 fewer than than 500 Vermonters listed mining and quarrying as their occupations.
VERMONT HISTORICAL SOCIETY PHOTOS

CHAPTER THREE

VERMONT'S ECOLOGY

Ecological change is usually so gradual, and a human life so brief, that one seldom witnesses a natural transformation as radical and extensive as that of Vermont's landscape. Yet many old-timers have seen the changes from their own yards. The surrounding forested hillsides once were meadows and pastures; in the 1880s as much as 80 percent of the state was cleared for farming. Today the proportions are reversed. Not surprisingly, Vermont's ecological communities have been influenced and changed drastically as well.

Under natural conditions Vermont is covered with trees. The liberal amounts of year-round precipitation and the infrequency of catastrophic fires allow forests to outcompete other vegetative types like grasses and shrubs that dominate more arid parts of the U.S. Though natural wildfires were rare, human-ignited blazes were common— at least at lower elevation. Indians of New England burned the trees to clear fields. Sometimes thousands of acres were charred by runaway conflagrations, leaving entire mountains barren of forest for decades. This accounts for the ubiquitous "Bald Mountain" in the region, named by white settlers who took note of the treeless condition of the peaks.

The Indians also burned vegetation from the drier areas to concentrate deer and other wildlife in the swamps and wet lowlands where the fires could not penetrate. Hunting was easier since animals were not as widely dispersed as they are today. In areas densely populated by Indians, such as along the New England coast, the land was burned lightly, but repeatedly, and early settlers frequently commented on how easy it was to ride a horse through these open and park-like forests without the aid of a trail or path. Early accounts tell of a patchwork of meadows and oak and hickory forests around Lake Champlain resulting from Indian-set fires, but most of Vermont's forests were thicker and much more continuous than those to the south and east.

Like slash-and-burn farmers in the tropical rainforests, New England Indians used a field for a few years before the soil, wood (used for cooking and warming fires), and local game populations were depleted. Fields the Indians abandoned quickly reverted to forest.

The Indian way disappeared quickly when white settlers arrived. The European system of fixed boundaries and settled villages was incompatible with a slash-and-burn agricultural system. Instead each family cut its own plot of land from the forested slopes and tilled the soil year after year. To clear the forest in the days before the chain saw and bulldozer was backbreaking, tedious work, accomplished with axes. Stumps were pulled from the ground with horses, and the slash piled and burned. Grazing, plowing and mowing kept the land open, but if these activities ever ceased, the trees immediately swallowed the hard-earned fields.

Clearing the Forests

In the late 1800s, the forests that had escaped the farmers' original clearing were attacked with ax and saw

Maidenhair fern in the Green Mountains is indicative of the humid climate that prevails in Vermont during summer months.
GEORGE WUERTHNER

Facing page, right: Sphagnum moss on the forest floor in the Green Mountains. This moss has two types of cells. Live ones near the surface manufacture food, while dead subsurface cells act as water reservoirs. Indians took advantage of the plant's absorptive quality by using it for diapers. GEORGE WUERTHNER
Left: Red raspberry. TED LEVIN

GREEN MOUNTAIN NATIONAL FOREST

Running like a backbone down the entire length of the state, the Green Mountain range provides a beautiful, inspiring backdrop for Vermont's villages and towns. The Green Mountain National Forest encompasses more than half of the range, and is split into two disjunct units. The south unit runs from the Massachusetts border north to Wallingford; the north unit starts near Rutland and reaches up to Waitsfield. Many of the state's high peaks lie within the boundaries of the forest, and the Long Trail runs its length. In addition to numerous recreational opportunities, including hunting, fishing, skiing and wilderness camping in five designated wilderness areas, the forest provides watershed stability and wildlife habitat that has been increasingly eroded from the state's private lands.

The Green Mountain National Forest is the only national forest in Vermont and the largest piece of federal land in the state. Public lands are scarce in Vermont. Early land grants partitioned the entire state into towns, and nearly all of Vermont's 9,276 square miles once were privately owned. In 1905, when the federal Forest Service was established, Vermont had no public land base from which a national forest could be created.

In the same year the Forest Service was organized, a forward-thinking mill operator and timberland owner named Marshel J. Hapgood began a movement to bring a national forest into existence in Vermont. Though a logger himself, Hapgood was dismayed by the forestry practices of his day. Instead of clearcutting, Hapgood advocated a radical new approach to forestry then being developed, which called for selective cutting of individual trees. This technique limited soil erosion and other negative ecological impacts. (Ironically, the very forestry practice he sought to curb—clearcutting—now is the dominant timber harvest method used on public lands.)

Shortly after the Forest Service was established, Hapgood offered to sell his property at a very low price to the federal government, hoping that this would be incentive to place a national forest in Vermont's Green Mountains. Unfortunately, the law that had established the new federal agency had not included provisions for government purchase of private lands to create a national forest. Hapgood's offer had to be rejected.

In 1910, another Vermonter named Joseph Battell considered donating 30,000 acres of Green Mountain property either to the state, federal government or his alma mater, Middlebury College. With no federal forest system in Vermont, Battell eventually gave the majority of his land to Middlebury.

The Weeks Act was passed in 1911, and gave the federal government the power to buy private land for national forest establishment. Soon after the act became law, Vermont citizens led by Senator Frank Greene began to lobby Congress for creation of a Green Mountain National Forest. As a result of these efforts, the Forest Service began a review to determine if any areas met the criteria set by the Weeks Act. In 1920 two places were identified—the 340,000-acre Nulhegan Unit in the Northeast Kingdom, and a 100,000-acre southern unit centered in Bennington and Windham counties. Although the Forest Service agreed that these areas met the legal requirements, they concluded that other parts of the country were in greater need of federal attention.

The federal government's rejection of Vermont as a suitable region for a new forest prompted even greater lobbying and organizational efforts. The Vermont legislature passed the Enabling Act for the much-desired forest, inviting the federal service to reconsider the Green Mountain National Forest proposal. Other groups including the Vermont Forestry Association and Green Mountain Club urged the Forest Service to review its decision.

After the devastating floods of 1927, a new sense of urgency was given to protection of mountain watersheds. Governor John Weeks officially requested that a national forest be established in Vermont. The Vermont Commissioner of Forestry presented a formal proposal to the federal government, not only emphasizing the benefits a national forest would have for the wood industry, but also outlining the attractions that federal lands would have for recreationists in the heavily-populated eastern U.S. The latter advantage finally convinced federal authorities of the need for a national forest in Vermont. In 1932, after four years of study that resulted in new boundary recommendations, President Herbert Hoover signed the proclamation creating the Green Mountain National Forest. Eventually the boundaries for federal acquisition were set at 629,000 acres within two units. By 1986, 325,400 acres were under federal ownership. And at last Hapgood's and Battell's visions were made reality. The government, under the Weeks Act, was able to take Hapgood's property under its wing; Middlebury College sold the land given it by Battell.

Ironically, though Vermonters had lobbied strongly for the establishment of the new forest, once the legislation was enacted and land acquisition began, a new wave of anti-federal feelings arose among many rural residents. Most state officials and many prominent citizens approved of the new national forest, but local inhabitants feared federal control over what they considered their personal domain. Some towns worried about the loss of tax dollars if private lands were passed into public ownership. The Weeks Act required the federal government to pay townships within the boundaries of the forest 25 percent of its gross receipts from logging, recreation, and grazing fees. The limited economic activity during the Depression of the 1930s, however, resulted in small federal payments to affected communities. Anxiety levels in those towns rose. In addition, a tradition of anti-big-government, anti-centralization sentiment among many Vermonters led them to interpret the national forest system as just another manifestation of "creeping socialism." In the era of President Franklin Roosevelt's New Deal, there seemed to be all too much of that already.

Adding fuel to the fire was a National Park Service proposal to build a Green Mountain Skyline Parkway similar to the Blue Ridge Parkway that was eventually bulldozed through the southern Appalachians. The proposed highway would have required the purchase of 35,000 acres of land, as well as the construction of campgrounds and trails. Vermonters hotly contested the parkway and in 1935 the Vermont House of Representatives went on record opposing the project. Nevertheless, the state's governor, noting the economic gains to be had from the federally-funded road, asked that the proposal be reconsidered. Eventually, in a state-wide referendum, the Vermont voters vetoed the scenic highway 42,318 to 30,897.

Although the Green Mountain National Forest has purchased approximately half the private lands within its legislated boundaries, it has become increasingly difficult for the federal government to gain the requisite approval of some local governments. The rising tide of rural recreational development makes private lands near the national forest particularly attractive and valuable for second homes. Tax income to local communities from these condo and vacation home sites is potentially much higher than the 25-percent revenue sharing provided by the federal government.

Today less than 5 percent of Vermont is under the jurisdiction of the Green Mountain National Forest, yet the public benefits are multiplying yearly. Much of the state's perceived high quality of life hinges on its rural, undeveloped landscape and access to those lands. As more and more private property is posted and closed to the public, the small amount of government-owned land has to fill the void for those seeking outdoor recreation opportunities. A substantial amount of the state's wildlife habitat also exists on private lands, but suburban growth as well as recreation development threatens these areas, and wildlife habitat preservation will increasingly fall to the public sector. In addition, long-term comprehensive land management is difficult to organize and coordinate on private parcels because ownership is divided among many individuals and companies who have multitudinous goals and purposes. Even those with the wish to preserve their properties in a natural state are usually limited in their financial ability to do so. Finally, only the federal lands have the legal commitment to preserve large tracts of land for their long-term ecological stability. As Vermont's population continues to grow, federal lands may be the only areas left where such preservation is realized.

In the crowded northeastern U.S., a region with extremely limited public land opportunities, national forest lands are a priceless treasure. Perhaps in recognition of this role, the recently completed Green Mountain National Forest Plan has reversed a policy of managing its lands for commodity production— such as timber harvest— in favor of a new emphasis on recreation and preservation of the non-commodity resources such as wildlife habitat.

Above: Although the Green Mountain National Forest was created to protect watersheds, it has become increasingly important for recreation, especially as more and more private lands are posted against trespass.

Facing page: Moss Glen Falls in Green Mountain National Forest. GEORGE WUERTHNER PHOTOS

This old photo of Montpelier shows the deforestation of the surrounding slopes during the last century.
VERMONT HISTORICAL SOCIETY
Facing page, right: Although most of Vermont is reforested, most trees are young, like these maples.
JAMES RANDKLEV
Left: Paper birch is one of the first trees to colonize a field or burn and grows rapidly but cannot tolerate shade. If left undisturbed, birch is eventually replaced by more shade-tolerant species. GEORGE WUERTHNER

a burned or cut-over region. Aspen seedlings can survive only in open areas and seldom are found under dense forest canopies, thus as the forest closes in, the sun-loving aspen is gradually replaced— barring any further disruption— by species more tolerant of shade, such as sugar maple. This sequential, gradual replacement of one species with another is called succession. How predictable the series is depends on a host of factors including soil type, climatic trends, availability of seed sources, the competition between species and the influence of other biotic factors such as browsing deer. Each factor plays a part in the determination of what plant species grows where.

The forest we now see in Vermont probably is not the same forest that existed at the time of settlement. Some species were adversely affected by the advent of European man; elm, for example, has virtually disappeared as a result of accidental introduction of the Dutch elm disease from Europe, while other species such as sugar maple may have increased, filling the ecological void left by the declining species.

Much of early Vermont was covered with coniferous forest or a mixed forest of pine and hardwoods— below 2,500' stately old-growth white pine were particularly abundant. In colonial times these ramrod trees were valuable for ship building, especially favored for masts. The king of England proclaimed ownership of all pines in the colonies more than 24" in diameter, and sent agents to enforce the regulation. This edict infuriated the early settlers who looked upon local natural resources as their own. This regulation contributed to the colonists' discontent with English rule and fueled their revolutionary fervor. The law was difficult to enforce and many colonial-period homes were built with pine planks only 23" wide— always cut from trees just under the 24" limit. After the American Revolution white pine became the major lumber species sought by loggers and the tree was so heavily harvested that it nearly disappeared from the landscape. It was only in the 20th century that white pine again began to recover from this period of free-wheeling timber harvest.

White pine readily colonizes open areas such as recently burned land or abandoned fields. Thus, the rectangular patches of pine one often sees on hillsides or at the base of mountains represent former clearings. Loggers selectively cut the pines while leaving behind hardwoods— this is one reason hardwoods dominate in Vermont today. As a pioneer species, white pine will, over hundreds of years, be replaced on the better, moister sites by the more shade-tolerant hardwoods, but

for lumber and pulp. Even the highest peaks were cut over and the logs floated down rivers or moved by rail to the mills. Great log drives were an annual event on the Connecticut and other rivers of the state. The overall result was the obliteration of nearly all of Vermont's virgin forest, and though much of the state is reforested, the absence of large, mature trees is a noticeable feature of these woodlands.

Recolonization of abandoned fields or cut-over forests follows a predictable sequence because of differences in the way each species responds to its environment. For example, quaking aspen is referred to as a pioneer species because it is often the first tree to invade

on droughty soils, it usually dominates indefinitely because the species' deep taproot allows it to reach moisture unavailable to other species.

While white pine colonizes open areas, eastern hemlock, another conifer, is almost always a tree of shady, moist nooks and crannies along lake shores and streambanks, and in wooded glens. Its high tolerance for shade enables it to grow well under a hardwood canopy. Hemlock groves make superior winter deer yards since the dense cover of the trees gives the animals a refuge from wind and deep snow. Hemlock also is very palatable winter food for deer. Unfortunately, with the high deer populations of recent decades heavy browsing on

Top: Fern fronds in spring. TED LEVIN

Above: Conifers dominate timberline sites on Vermont's higher peaks. Common species include red spruce, balsam fir and hardy hardwood species like mountain paper birch. Baker Peak—Green Mountains. GEORGE WUERTHNER

hemlock has drastically reduced the young seedlings and saplings of this species in many parts of the state.

Hemlock prefers cool but not cold sites, and reaches its northern limit in southern and central Vermont. In cold regions of the state, such as the Northeast Kingdom or at higher elevations in the mountains, one is more likely to encounter spruce, of which there are three species in Vermont— red, black and white. Red spruce is the most widespread of the three and its great tolerance of harsh, cold conditions makes it a common species of the state's higher elevations.

The harsh environmental conditions found at timberline— around 4,000' in Vermont's mountains— force both spruce and balsam fir, another common high-elevation species, to assume a sprawling, stunted, twisted form. Krummholz, which means "crooked wood" in German, is the result of wind, ice-particle abrasion and a short growing season. Many of these dwarf trees appear to have been trimmed like hedges. Their even height marks the average winter snow depth. Above the snow, the wind severely abrades exposed branches.

Since life at timberline is at best, a marginal venture, any new stress placed on the region's forests is likely to first show up here. Not surprisingly, the initial indications that air pollution was adversely affecting New England's woodlands were documented on Camel's Hump, where it was noted that red spruce were inexplicably dying. Research by faculty at the University of Vermont demonstrated a significant decline in total number of trees as well as in seedling survival among red spruce, sugar maple, balsam fir, beech and mountain maple. No single factor could be identified as the sole culprit in this complex problem, but strong circumstantial evidence suggests that the combined effects of acidic rain, heavy metals and other wind-blown pollutants are precipitating the die-off on Camel's Hump as well as affecting the forest cover throughout New England.

Northern white cedar also is restricted to a particular soil. This species favors calcareous soils along Lake Champlain and Grand Isle. The graceful cedars overhanging the lakeshore are a distinctive feature of this region.

Hardwood Forests

A common hardwood in Vermont, and certainly the easiest to recognize, is the paper birch, which takes its name from the white, peeling bark that resembles strips of parchment. This species, intolerant of shade, is common all across the boreal forest stretching from Maine to Alaska. With aspen, it is one of the first trees to recolonize burned areas. Indians preferred to cover their canoes with the bark of paper birch because it is waterproof, peels in large pieces, and is abundant throughout the region. Repair or replacement of damaged segments was also easy. Since paper birch is better adapted to cool climates and short growing seasons than most hardwoods, the variety known as mountain paper birch is a common associate of red spruce and balsam fir at timberline.

The most common hardwood species in Vermont is the sugar maple. In autumn its fiery leaves constitute one of the main ingredients in autumn's chromatographic display. Unlike paper birch, sugar maple is not hindered by shade. Thus, as a forest approaches climax— beyond which no further change in forest type occurs— the proportion of sugar maple increases.

Another climax hardwood is American beech. Since it is shallow-rooted, it requires fairly moist, but not saturated, sites. Beech trees, like aspen, sprout suckers from their roots and quickly spread into any vacant area in the forest. Their triangular nuts are an important food for wildlife; deer paw through shallow snow to feed on them.

Other common species that grow with sugar maple and beech are yellow birch, black cherry, red maple, basswood and white ash. In wet lowlands grow balsam poplar, silver maple, eastern cottonwood and black ash.

Some plant species reach their northern, eastern or southern limits in Vermont. For example, plants adapted to milder climates such as flowering dogwood, black gum, sycamore and mountain laurel all find habitat in Vermont's low-elevation areas, including the lower Connecticut River Valley, southwest Vermont near Pownal, and near Lake Champlain— although the distribution of any particular species may be restricted to just one of these areas.

Oaks, including the black, red and white species found throughout the Midwest and southern New England, are uncommon in Vermont and restricted primarily to the warmer, drier spots and are most common in the Lake Champlain lowlands. Their acorns are an important wildlife food wherever oaks are found, but a forest survey conducted in 1973 found that only 3.5 percent of Vermont's commercial forestland was of the oak-pine or oak-hickory type.

Plants reaching their southern limits in Vermont are mostly alpine and arctic in origin. The state contains only two small patches of true alpine tundra: 250 acres on Mt. Mansfield and another 10 acres on Camel's

Hump to the south. These are remnants of the Ice Age, isolated on Vermont's mountain tops by the upwardly advancing forests that developed since the retreat of the last continental glacier. Growing here are species also at home on the tundra in northern Alaska, including purple mountain saxifrage, Lapland diapensia and black crowberry. The plants grow in small clumps nestled close to the ground where they are sheltered from the worst environmental extremes of temperature and wind.

The change from forest to open fields and back to hardwood forest is one conspicuous example of ecological change over time. However, other less apparent alterations have occurred as well, including the extirpation of some of the state's wildlife species.

The Animal Kingdom

Many animals at the edge of their geographical range and living in marginal habitat were eliminated early. Boreal forest residents such as caribou and wolverine no doubt wandered through the spruce-fir forests of the Northeast Kingdom, but disappeared shortly after white settlement. Lynx, marten, mountain lion and wolf were all present in good numbers but were eliminated by excessive hunting, trapping and habitat loss. Occasional reports of these species are most likely misidentifications or random wanderings of single animals from other states as no breeding populations are known to occur here.

Some species like the Atlantic salmon— once common in the Connecticut River and its tributaries— slowly are making a tenuous comeback. Two factors, logging (which caused stream sedimentation) and dams (which blocked spawning runs) combined to nearly exterminate the salmon, but habitat improvements and a major restocking effort have seen incremental victories. Spawning fish now reach as far upstream as the White River, which empties into the Connecticut at White River Junction.

Although today the whitetail-deer population is quite healthy, it was nearly exterminated from the state. The main culprits were extensive deforestation due to the agricultural expansion of the 1800s and overhunting. In 1878, 17 whitetail deer were trapped in New York state and released in Vermont in an attempt to rescue the state's declining herd. The implementation of strictly enforced hunting regulations and the reforestation of a large percentage of the state brought about the population's rapid recovery and by 1970 it had grown to well over 150,000 animals.

WHY LEAVES CHANGE COLOR

Maple leaves. SONJA BULLATY

The annual autumn foliage display of brilliant golds, russets and reds is the result of a complex interaction of weather, day length and hormones in the trees. In order to protect themselves from the advancing winter, the trees transfer their energy reserves from the leaves to the roots and other storage areas. This not only establishes a store of energy on which the tree can draw the following spring, but also reduces the amount of water the tree loses. Deciduous-tree leaves are inefficient at conserving water (conifers are much better), thus as the soil freezes it becomes impossible for the roots to replace water lost through the leaf surface. Rather than continue to lose non-replaceable water, the tree goes into dormancy.

Chlorophyll is the pigment that makes leaves green. It employs sunlight energy to photochemically produce sugars— the basic food for the tree's growth and maintenance. Chlorophyll is cold-sensitive and breaks down as temperatures drop below freezing for any period of time. As cool autumn weather with its frosty nights moves in, the leaves on deciduous trees stop producing new chlorophyll. The orange and yellow pigments called carotenoids, previously masked by the chlorophyll, become prominent. Also, sugars begin to accumulate in the leaves and activate the production of red and purple pigments called anthocyanins. This is especially true in the bright scarlet leaves of some oaks and maples.

Eventually, the prolonged colder temperatures reduce the production of hormones that keep the leaves attached to the stem. The attachment points weaken and the leaves flutter to the earth. In some trees, such as oaks, the leaves are high in tannins, which cause the leaves to brown and remain hanging on the tree.

Moose were eliminated from Vermont during the 1800s but have slowly recolonized the state. They are susceptible to a parasite that causes disorientation and even death, but according to a recent study the greatest mortality comes from poaching and car collisions.

A barred owl, a common forest dweller. TED LEVIN PHOTOS

The natural northern range of the whitetail ends in Vermont; at higher latitudes the snows are too deep and winters too long for the deer to survive. Crucial to their survival are their winter "yards" which usually consist of mature coniferous forests whose dense canopies block wind and heavy snowfall. Suitable winter habitat is often at some distance from summer range; it also is more limited in extent. The availability of winter yarding areas is the ultimate determinant of the land's potential to support them.

The return of Vermont's forests after the turn of the century brought about a renewal of prime deer habitat and assured the recovery of the state's populations. In fact, deer are so fecund that by the 1950s and '60s the herds had grown beyond the land's carrying capacity. Periodic, massive die-offs resulted and the Fish and Game department attempted to institute an antlerless deer season to reduce the herds. But public opinion would not allow it. Vermonters were, by then, used to the large herds and believed that hunting the does would destroy the herds. Range conditions continued to deteriorate and, stressed by poor nutrition, the deer died by the thousands during the severe winters between 1969 and 1971. The population was halved. More deer expired from this devastating famine than were ever killed during the hunting season.

Deer can replace their numbers quite rapidly and readily, however, so the herds began to recover almost immediately. But the plant communities continued to be ravaged. Deer can recoup their losses in a matter of years, but an overbrowsed range takes decades to come back. Despite proof that in other states the does had been regularly and successfully harvested for years, Vermont's hunters resisted adoption of any new regulations. Furthermore, final policy decisions rested with the legislature, not the Fish and Game department. Politicians, not biologists, dictated wildlife management. Finally, in 1979, Fish and Game was granted responsibility for deer regulation. It promptly instituted a doe season amid much protest. It's still too early to determine whether the department's actions will ultimately aid deer habitat, but the evidence from other states indicates that Vermont is following sound biological reasoning, if not good political policy.

It is clear why public approval and cooperation are so crucial to the work of state biologists and proper wildlife management. In 1985, 115,713 deer licenses were sold—96,351 of them to residents. This is approximately one-fifth of the state's population! When one considers that most women, children and old people are not hunters, it becomes apparent that an overwhelming majority of Vermont's able-bodied men and boys participate in the annual autumn rite. The total legal deer kill in 1985 was 13,877 animals— or about one tenth of the state's estimated deer population.

Whitetail deer carry a parasitic roundworm that is non-debilitating to them, but which can cause neurological problems and even death in moose. Over evolutionary time, the deer's tolerance of roundworm has allowed it to expand into habitat that might otherwise be occupied by moose. With the growth of Vermont's deer herds, this has meant the accompanying spread of the roundworm, via the whitetail's feces, to moose ranges. Once the roundworm is excreted by the deer, a land snail, which then acquires the parasite, plays the role of intermediate host. The moose then ingests the snails on the leaves and pond vegetation they normally consume. Once inside the moose, the worm bores into the moose's brain tissue and lays its eggs. The larvae hatch there and move into the bloodstream. Once they reach the digestive tract they are eliminated from the body to begin the cycle again. A severely infected moose is disoriented and uncoordinated. Occasionally, moose are found in cow pastures or even walking down village streets. This unusual behavior is most often a sign of an advanced stage of the disease.

Due to the large deer herd die-offs of the 1970s, moose populations received a slight reprieve. Moose numbers began to rise from an estimated 25 individuals in the early 1960s to 200 or more by 1980. The swelling population began to alarm hunters who believed the deer herds would be diminished as a consequence. Today moose are found throughout the Northeast Kingdom and are scattered through remote areas of the Green Mountains such as around Groton, Ripton, Somerset, Waterbury, Wallingford and Eden.

In 1980 the Fish and Game department initiated a four-year study to determine the range and status of moose in Vermont. Although the animals are increasing in number, it appeared that a great deal of good moose habitat was not being utilized. The brain worm parasite was an immediate suspect, but surprisingly the researchers found a rather low incidence of the parasite. Only 14 percent of the moose examined were infected. Nonetheless, moose mortality was high: of the 38 moose checked by biologists, not one was older than $4^1/2$ years! In a normal, heathy population some moose should live into the teens. Upon further research, it was found that poachers— particularly in the Northeast Kingdom— and

collisions with cars were the major moose killers. The lack of older animals has serious implications, for female moose may not breed until they are at least $3^1/2$ years old. Older females are also more likely to successfully rear young. In the absence of serious brain worm infection, it seems that Vermont's moose populations is most restricted by human actions. In 1986, Fish and Game estimates placed the herd between 300 and 600 animals. Unless the unnaturally high mortality can be

White-tailed deer nearly were driven to extinction within the state by a combination of year-round hunting. and habitat loss as a result of agricultural development. In 1878, 17 deer were trapped in New York to bolster the animal's numbers in Vermont. Today an estimated 150,000 whitetails roam the state.
TED LEVIN

Top: *Short-tailed weasel in white winter coat.* TED LEVIN
Above: *River otters once were common throughout the state.* TED LEVIN

Facing page, top left: *The eastern coyote, first seen here in 1948, is larger than its western counterpart.* TED LEVIN
Top right: *Great blue herons nest in colonies near water.* TED LEVIN
Bottom left: *Sleek and fast, a peregrine falcon with a kill.* KENNAN WARD
Bottom right: *Pileated woodpeckers need large snags for nesting.* SCOTT NIELSEN

controlled, moose numbers will probably never climb much higher.

Another large animal that thus far has survived human intrusion is the black bear. Although their secretive ways make population estimates extremely unreliable, some 2,000 bears are thought to live in Vermont. When one considers that the bear carried a bounty until 1941, trapped until 1967, and still is hunted with dogs, it seems incredible indeed that they are not extinct here like fellow carnivores— the wolves and mountain lions. About 200 bears are killed each year; the largest ever taken in Vermont weighed an estimated 470 pounds.

Although black bears were killed because they were feared and undesirable, other animals— such as the otter, fisher, beaver and marten— were the victims of their attractiveness and utility to man. Their beautiful pelts were extremely valuable and the search for furs prompted the first white explorations into what is now Vermont. As early as 1660, French Canadians were trading rifles, knives and axes with local Indians in exchange for the precious skins. The Indians trapped the beaver into near-extinction even before white settlement. Then, the few animals remaining were further pressed by habitat destruction following human in-migration. By 1853 Zadock Thompson could write in his book, Natural History of Vermont, "The beaver, though formerly a very common animal in Vermont, is probably nearly or quite exterminated, none of them having been killed within the state, to my knowledge, for several years." In a belated effort to save whatever animals survived in the state, the legislature gave the beaver full protection in 1910. Again, reforestation after the turn of the century abetted beaver recovery and the animals gradually began to reestablish themselves in the Northeast Kingdom. In an effort to speed up the process, reintroductions were made in Bennington County in 1921, in Caledonia County in 1932, and around Peacham in 1937. From these small beginnings beaver have reclaimed rivers and ponds all across the state. In 1985 alone, trappers took more than 2,603 of the industrious, large rodents.

The fisher, too, a large weasel-like furbearer, was reintroduced to the state between 1957 and 1967. It is one of the few predators, along with mountain lions, that eats porcupines regularly. The prickly beasts themselves dine on bark, as well as wooden buildings, and are thus considered pests by the timber industry, woodlot and property owners. To control the porkies, the state brought 124 fisher from Maine to Vermont woods. In 1974, the fisher population had rebounded to the point that they could be legally trapped. By 1985 more than 4,161 fisher had been killed, with 612 the highest number taken in any one year.

Unfortunately, the stories of the marten and lynx do not have such happy endings. Marten are inhabitants of mature forest. Trapping combined with the land clearing of the 18th and 19th centuries eliminated them from the state's fauna. The lynx, larger relative of the bobcat, also is gone.

The wild turkey, symbol of our Thanksgiving tradition, was eliminated from Vermont by the mid-1800s for much the same reasons— habitat loss and uncontrolled hunting. In 1968, the Fish and Game department began a program to bring back the turkey. Seventeen birds were trapped in southwestern New York and released in Pawlet, on the western Vermont border. The next winter, 14 more were captured and reintroduced near Castleton. By 1973 an estimated 600 turkeys resided in the state. To reestablish the gobblers on the eastern side of the state, descendents of the original transplants were trapped and trucked across the Green Mountains, where they were released in Windham County. Wild turkeys are now found at lower elevations throughout southern Vermont and extend all the way to the Canadian border along the Lake Champlain lowlands. In 1973 the first turkey hunting season in more than a hundred years netted 23 birds. By 1985 the statewide kill from both the spring and fall season totaled 1,302 birds.

Fish and Fowl—Healthy or in Danger

Work to restore Atlantic salmon to the Connecticut River has been a major program in New England for two decades. This river once had one of the largest runs of this anadromous (sea-roaming) fish on the continent. The ambitious project has involved improvement and re-creation of salmon spawning habitat as well as restocking. By 1985, 1,350 salmon had returned to the Connecticut River to spawn.

The spawning run occurs between April and July with the peak in mid-May to mid-June. The mature fish average 10 pounds. By October the salmon are on spawning beds in the upper reaches of the river drainage, which includes the West and the White rivers in Vermont. Here each female will lay as many as 10,000 eggs in gravel beds called redds. The eggs hatch the following spring and the young salmon emerge from the gravel in May or June. They feed in the tributary streams for a full year; those that survive predation and other hazards will begin their seaward journey the following spring. After entering the ocean, the fish migrate to Davis Strait off the coast of Greenland. Along the way, further inroads on their numbers are made by ocean predators. Also, commercial fishing takes a major portion, accounting for 50 percent or more of the potential Connecticut River salmon run. Those that escape the nets eventually make their way back to the river, swimming upstream to spawn and complete the cycle.

While the salmon gradually is returning to Vermont's rivers, another fascinating, much-admired creature is being reintroduced to Green Mountain skies. Peregrine falcons are sleek, fast-flying birds of prey that capture other birds on the wing. Prior to World War II, peregrines were relatively common in Vermont and there were at least 27 known occupied sites. But unrestricted use of pesticides wrought havoc on the peregrine and other birds at the top of the food chain. Pesticide residues in the body tissues of their prey were further concentrated in their own systems. The toxic chemicals caused the birds to produce fragile and thin-shelled eggs that frequently broke before the young could hatch. The last wild peregrine in Vermont was seen in 1970 and the species was probably extinct in the eastern United States shortly thereafter. Using birds captured in the West and the Arctic, researchers at Cornell University began to raise captive birds and release them in the wild. As of 1985 more than 700 young, lab-hatched birds had been released, but mortality is high and only 16 pairs are known to have survived to adulthood and successfully raise young. One pair nested on the cliffs overlooking Lake Willoughby and their offspring were the first peregrines known to have hatched in Vermont since 1957. While it's still too early to determine whether the peregrine will ever fully recover from its near-extinction, the Lake Willoughby pair and other successes give wildlife enthusiasts reason to hope that one day, without continuing need of human assistance, these splendid birds again will fly Vermont skies.

Wildlife Management

The recovery of nearly all of these species has required direct human intervention, but one animal not only has established itself in Vermont without any assistance from people, it has done so in spite of widespread, though unfounded, fear and hostility toward it. This plucky beast is the eastern coyote. It has inhabited eastern North America only within the last half to three quarters of a century. None was known in Vermont until 1948. Apparently, they expanded eastward from their original western range following the extirpation of wolves

LOONS

If you're lucky, on a quiet spring evening you may hear the haunting "yodel" of the common loon as it drifts along the surface of a northern Vermont lake, between strands of mist. The common loon is found all across Canada and northern states like Montana, Minnesota and Maine. Long associated with wilderness settings and the "North Country," loons inhabit only a handful of Vermont lakes and their numbers may be declining. In 1986 only 12 pairs of the strikingly beautiful black and white birds were known to nest in the state and only 17 chicks were successfully fledged. The bird has been recommended for listing on the state's Endangered Species List.

Loons are a primitive water bird, not too distantly removed from reptiles, the evolutionary ancestors of all birds. Unlike its more highly evolved avian relatives, the loon does not have hollow bones and hence has trouble getting airborne. Its distinctive take-off— running wildly across the water's surface, wings flapping, feet pumping, neck extended— is one result of its heavy skeleton.

But the dense bones also give the loon a specific gravity near that of water, and thus aid it in diving. Compressing air beneath its feathers and expelling it from air sacs in its body cavity, the loon can decrease its specific gravity and thus sink lower into the water.

The loon feeds primarily on fish, usually capturing prey by outswimming it. The bird's muscular legs are attached far back on the body and only the ankle bone and feet are capable of free movement. It thus gets powerful unidirectional propulsion. In addition, the wings are very small for a bird of its size, resulting in reduced drag underwater and adding to its flying difficulties. Even with vigorous flapping, most loons need 300' to 400' of "runway" just to get off the water. This may be one reason they are never found on tiny ponds or potholes—they would be permanently grounded!

Because its legs are positioned so far back on the body, the loon has a very difficult time walking on land. In fact, it could hardly be said to walk at all. Instead it rests on its breast and pushes itself along with its legs— a decidedly comical performance. Water landings are no more graceful. Due to the limited lift provided by its tiny wings, once a loon stops flapping, it practically falls from the sky to crash unceremoniously with a gliding splash onto the water.

Loons usually return year

Common loon numbers are declining in Vermont. To help the loon and other species, the state recently enacted legislation that allows taxpayers to contribute money from their income tax returns to support Vermont's non-game species program, which funds research and management.
DANIEL J. COX

after year to the same lake to nest, arriving just after or someimes even before the ice has gone out. Courtship and territorial displays are spectacular. The males bow, splash and dance on the water, yodeling all the while to mark out their territories. A mated pair constructs a nest of reeds and other vegetation or may scoop out a shallow depression in the soil. The nest site is on or near the water, in quiet secluded coves or on islands. The female usually lays two eggs and both parents share in the incubation duties, which last 28 to 29 days.

Human activities pose the greatest threat to the loon's continued survival in Vermont. Lakeshore development, which destroys the quiet secluded coves and bays, is one threat. But even

casual recreation activities like canoeing, motor boating, water skiing, swimming and fishing can distract or disturb the loons to the point that they will abandon the nest during incubation, or separate from the vulnerable chicks. Fluctuations in water levels also can precipitate reproductive failure.

One of the loon's major predators is the raccoon. If the parents are disturbed during incubation and are forced to leave the nest for even a short period of time, the opportunistic raccoon frequently will consume the untended eggs. Lakeshore development, which includes campgrounds and cottages, has increased the availability of human garbage, and thus the numbers of raccoons, in or near loon nesting habitat.

Loon populations are especially vulnerable to any decrease because of their low reproductive capacity. Adults do not breed until they are at least four years of age, and usually only two eggs are produced per mated pair in a single nesting season. In addition, although baby loons are precocious youngsters and able to swim less than 24 hours after hatching, they remain dependent upon their parents for food and protection for nearly 12 weeks. Juvenile Vermont loons are sufficiently developed to fly by September, and sometime in mid-October they begin their southward migration to spend the winters in salt-water coastal areas along the East Coast.

in the East and later the Midwest and the Great Plains. The coyotes moved into the ecological niche vacated by their larger cousins. Interestingly, in regions where wolves live, coyotes are either absent or few in numbers. There is some competition and dietary overlap between the two species. This eastern breed of coyote is heavier and less streamlined than its western ancestors and biologists suspect that some interbreeding with wolves occurred during the eastward migration. A large male eastern coyote will sometimes weigh up to 50 pounds— just 10 to 20 pounds less than the average weight of wolves in Minnesota.

In all likelihood, one factor contributing to the coyote's expansion into Vermont has been the 20th century recovery of the whitetail deer herds. While a pack of coyotes is certainly able to pull down a deer, and does so on occasion, deer are more likely to be consumed as carrion— after the animals have died from starvation, for example, or from being hit by a car. These already-dead deer are important to the coyote's winter diet. But a far greater proportion of its day to day subsistence includes small rodents, snowshoe hares, rabbits, woodchucks, grouse and other small game.

With the advent of modern wildlife management, regeneration of the forest and preservation efforts begun around the turn of the century, many of Vermont's wildlife species have been able to make remarkable comebacks. But the work is not yet complete. Some species, such as the peregrine falcon and Atlantic salmon, still waver on the edge of extinction. Others, like the lynx, wolf and marten have yet to be returned to the state. Until the populations of all these species are secured, the recovery of Vermont's fauna will be unfinished.

Even the most concerted, dedicated efforts at preservation are ultimately doomed unless the continual disruption and development of wildlife habitat is controlled. As shopping centers, malls, condos and suburbs creep outward over the land, the natural landscape is fragmented into tiny useless pieces or eliminated entirely, often permanently. This shrinking habitat base endangers not only a single species, but the entire framework of biological and abiotic feedback systems which we call an ecosystem. Although we have laws to protect threatened species, we have yet to devise an adequate way to identify and save endangered ecosystems.

Top left: The fisher, once extinct in Vermont, was successfully reintroduced and now is trapped. TED LEVIN

Above: The wild turkey also became extinct in Vermont, but was successfully reintroduced and now ranges throughout southern Vermont, and north to the Canadian border along the Lake Champlain lowlands.
TED LEVIN

Left: An estimated 2,000 black bears inhabit the state. DANIEL J. COX

39

CHAPTER FOUR

CLIMATE

There are cold and blustery Vermont winter days when even the low-lying clouds are too miserable to snow. An old Yankee is accustomed to this "sour" sort of weather, however, and more than one observer has remarked on Vermonters' corresponding dispositions. Certainly endless weeks of gray sky do little to inspire perky chatter. The reason for this dour state character—climactic, at least—is that Vermont lies directly in the path of several major storm tracks. Polar and tropical air masses frequently converge over the state, giving it unpredictable and variable (read "cloudy") weather.

In fact, Vermont has the distinction of being one of the cloudiest places in the United States. In November, only 9 percent of the days are clear. Even "gloomy" Seattle, Washington averages better than 10 percent sunshine during its wettest winter months. Only five major cities have more cloudy days than Burlington's 199; they are Portland, Eugene and Salem, Oregon, Seattle, and Binghamton, New York. Vermont is not a prime market for solar energy development!

Nevertheless, despite frequently overcast skies Vermont is endowed with delightfully distinct seasons. On occasion, a vigorous storm knocks things around a bit, but for the most part the state is spared the climatic excesses of other regions. Hurricanes, for example, may smash into the coast of Rhode Island and Connecticut, but peter out by the time they reach southern Vermont. Extreme cold may test Vermonters' stamina a few times during the winter, but frigid temperatures usually do not last for weeks on end as they can in the upper Midwest or the northern Great Plains. And though summer usually offers up a good dose of those hot, muggy "dog" days when one gets soaked with sweat just sitting still, overall, the warm weather temperatures are considerably cooler than, say, in New York City or Washington, D.C.

The Five Seasons

Vermonters claim their state has five seasons: spring, summer, fall, and winter...and "Mud Season." Many residents like the cool, crisp days of autumn best. Others rejoice in the vibrant burst of life that hits about mid-May. Some go wild for snow, and skiing. On one season, however, all will agree. Mud Season is Vermont's Purgatory. It comes at the end of winter, when the first

It is said that Vermont has five seasons—spring, summer, autumn, winter and mud season, which typically comes in late March and early April, making passage over dirt roads nearly impossible.
GEORGE WUERTHNER

Facing page, right: A rainy day near Hewettville. Vermont has one of the cloudiest climates in the United States, rivaling the Pacific Northwest in percentage of cloud-covered days. JEFF GNASS

Left: The leafless woods of winter give Vermonters views not possible in the summer and thus new perspectives of their neighborhoods.
GEORGE WUERTHNER

prolonged warm spell melts the snow, and then commences to thaw the ground. Dirt roads become quagmires and travel in many rural areas comes to a slippery halt. In fact, some cynics claim that Town Meeting Day, held in the first week of March, was deliberately scheduled to minimize the number of people who are able to attend.

The advance of spring brings lengthening days and the return of sounds and smells. Water trickles down every slope and the ground weeps with little rivulets. Bird calls fill the morning air, and geese often can be heard honking as they fly north during stormless nights. The aroma of warm earth, frozen all winter, begins to permeate the air. People emerge from their houses; they rake the greening lawns, ride their long-neglected bikes, haul out the fishing tackle and line the lakes and riverbanks.

Summer brings hazy, humid weather and thunderstorms. Grass grows high and is laid low by the blades of the hay mowers. The crickets' chirps in the evening seem

Fingers are quickly frozen when scraping ice from car windshields. Icy highways make travel treacherous and the salt spread to make driving safer makes autos rust faster. Winter, for many, is best spent inside huddled close to a fire.

But for others, winter is exhilarating. The crisp air and magic of bright blue skies draws them outside. The leafless woods are brighter than in summer and views hidden all year by vegetation can once again be seen. The snow covers logs and brush, making areas that are summertime jungles into accessible winter playgrounds. Recreationists enter on snowmobiles, skis and snowshoes. Finally, winter is synonymous with ski season—the busiest time of year for many businesses and towns.

Air Masses and Topography

The origins of the air masses that pass over Vermont have a lot to do with the weather it experiences. Most prevailing winds are from the west or south. Winds sliding into the state from the northwest usually hale from central Canada and bring with them dry, cool or cold weather, while air masses borne on southerly winds come from the Gulf of Mexico and carry moist, humid air responsible for much of the rain and snow that falls on the state. In winter an added weather phenomenon is the storm originating in the North Atlantic, known as the "Northeaster." These oceanic air masses bring wet snow and often dump the largest snowfalls of the season.

The interaction of these various air masses and storm tracks produces the variable weather so typical of the Green Mountain State. When a strong high-pressure air mass dips south out of Canada, Vermonters are treated to clear, but cool weather. If the high pressure system begins to weaken, a low-pressure air mass from the south may sweep into the state; cloudiness increases and temperatures rise. Along the boundary between the cold and warm air masses, precipitation falls. Eventually another high-pressure system moves into the state from the northwest and the weather clears again.

Vermont's uneven topography complicates these generalized weather patterns. Most of the state's mountains are at right angles to the major pathway of air movement across the state. They force air masses to rise and cool, which often leads to precipitation. Mountain slopes thus experience greater annual precipitation than nearby valleys. For example, the annual precipitation on Camel's Hump is 78", while Burlington in the lowlands to the west receives only 33.6".

to be synchronized with the flash of fireflies. Vermonters and out-of-state visitors soak in the easy joy of the outdoors by hiking, dipping in local lakes and swimming holes, or by simply finding a shady spot to picnic or sip a cold drink.

Autumn is perhaps the most magical and cherished time of year. The air is clean and crunchy, the mornings are frosty and cool but the afternoons are sunny and mild. Roadside stands sell pumpkins and apples, while leaf peepers converge on the state, following the up-to-the-minute foliage bulletins to get them to the most brilliant scenery at just the right time. Residents put up storm windows, cut and stack firewood, cover their flower beds with mulch. After the first hard frost, there is usually a brief spell of warm weather termed "Indian Summer," before the harsher winds of November blow the last leaves from the trees, and perhaps bring early snow.

By the end of November, winter has begun in earnest. For many, winter is a time of unpleasantness. There is snow to shovel off the walk and driveway.

As might be expected from this example, the highest towns and weather stations report the greatest annual precipitation. For example, Mt. Mansfield at 4,083' averages 73.9" a year—much of it as snow. Somerset at 2,080' is another high-elevation reporting station; it too has a large yearly average of 51.6". At lower elevations the annual averages are lower as well. Wilmington is at only 1,640' and receives 45.7" of precipitation, while St. Johnsbury at 711' is even drier with 34.7". As a rule, the most precipitation falls at the higher elevations in the mountains, and precipitation levels drop the farther north or lower in elevation one goes. Thus the Lake Champlain lowlands, in the rainshadow of the Adirondack and Green mountains, are the driest part of the state, while the southern Green Mountains, open to moisture-carrying storm tracks from the south, are among the wettest.

Although Vermont has plenty of topographical relief with which to wring moisture from the numerous clouds that shroud it, it is still the driest New England state. This is due to its inland location some distance from the moisture-producing ocean. Burlington's average precipitation of 33.6" is less than New York City's 44" and much less than Miami, Florida's 55".

Temperature patterns vary with location and time of year. The coldest temperatures are usually recorded year-round in the Northeast Kingdom, where the state record low (also a New England record) of -50° F was measured at Bloomfield on the upper Connecticut River. The warmest areas are in the southwest near Bennington and the southeast corner of the state at Vernon, where the state record high of 107° was set. In general, summer temperature averages are more or less uniform. For example, the July average for Bennington is 69°, while Newport up in the northern end of the state is only one degree colder at 68°. But in winter, the differences between north and south become more pronounced. The January average for Newport is 14° while Bennington is considerably warmer at 22°. Nevertheless this still is much colder than New York City with 32° or even Boston with 30°.

The length of the growing season varies considerably around the state and also from year to year. The longest growing season in Vermont is at Vernon in the Connecticut River valley, and the shortest is at Somerset which sits at 2,200' in elevation. An example of the rule that the higher one climbs the lower the temperature, Somerset has 83 days between the last frost of spring and the first nip of autumn. Due to the moderating influence of Lake Champlain, Burlington's growing

season is 150 days, while Bennington's is two weeks shorter—only 136 frost-free days. As might be expected, northern locations such as Bloomfield (113 days) and Enosburg Falls (115 days) have the shortest frost-free seasons in the state. In fact, Bloomfield holds the state record for the shortest season ever—59 days recorded in the summer of 1918. How does Vermont's gardening potential compare with other locations? Chicago's growing season is 198 days, Philadelphia's is 211.

Although cold air may settle in the valleys, on the average, the higher one climbs up a mountain, the cooler it becomes. The rule of thumb is that for every 1,000' gained in elevation, the temperature drops 3.5°. Thus, with all things equal, the temperature on Mt. Mansfield should be approximately 14° cooler than that in Burlington. The highest temperature ever recorded on Mt. Mansfield is 80°. This is one reason for the popularity of summit houses during the last century, when wealthy

Despite its northern location, Vermont has warm, humid summers that allow for a fairly long growing season—Burlington, moderated by the nearby waters of Lake Champlain, has a 150-day frost-free season. FRANK BALTHIS
Facing page, top: Although today most residents and visitors alike probably view snow as a winter hazard, in days past it served as a smooth highway after being compressed by a horse-drawn roller. VERMONT HISTORICAL SOCIETY
Bottom: Magic Mountain from the air. Vermont's ski areas are considered the best in the eastern United States, and the state's ski industry now employs far more people than agriculture. ROBERT PERRON

Vermont's greatest climatic disaster was the 1927 flood, seen here in a photo of Montpelier. The flood prompted, among other things, the creation of the Green Mountain National Forest as a means of protecting the state's watersheds from excessive timber harvest.
VERMONT HISTORICAL SOCIETY

urbanites visited the mountaintop lodges to escape the heat of the lowlands. Remnants of this era include the numerous roads that now climb to the top of Vermont's high peaks such as Mts. Equinox and Mansfield.

Waters Tame and Wild

Large bodies of water like Lake Champlain can also modify the local weather. In spring, the chill lake waters cool lakeside air temperatures and delay flowering in nearby orchards until after the chance for late season frosts is nil. Conversely, in the autumn the relatively warm lake waters delay the arrival of the first frosts and extend the growing season by as much as 30 days. This is one reason the Lake Champlain lowlands are the major fruit-growing region of the state.

Lake Champlain is so deep and large that it freezes over relatively late in the season, usually not until January if it freezes at all. Cold winds blowing across the lake may pick up heat from the open lake water and form fog or low clouds just east of the lake. The heavily overcast skies so common over Burlington (199 cloudy days a year) are partially the result of its proximity to the nearby lake.

The mountainous terrain also can influence wind patterns. High winds known colloquially as shirkshires occasionally flow down narrow valleys like the Valley of

Vermont near Bennington. Shirkshires develop when air masses are stalled by mountain barriers. Pressures build up enough to allow them to climb over the mountains and sweep down the far side. If this rush of air is further confined by a narrow valley, it can reach hurricane force.

The November 1927 Flood, which killed 84 people, is a prime example of how topography, in unison with regional storm patterns, can bring about a natural disaster. November 3, 1927 began as a wet, blustery day, but nothing seemed out of the ordinary in the gloomy early-winter morning. A weak storm, spawned in the mid-Atlantic Ocean was pushing into southern Vermont, and dropped light rains as it began to ascend the Green Mountains, but otherwise little rainfall was reported over the rest of the state. A cooler air mass that had moved in from the west was meanwhile stalled over western Vermont. With an air mass blocking its exit to the west, the mid-Atlantic storm should have moved northeast, out of the state and into the North Atlantic. But a dense, heavy mass of cold air had moved south from the Arctic to hover off the New England coast and block the northeasterly movement of the storm systems now centered over Vermont. As the relatively moist, warm air from the Atlantic encountered the colder air west of the Green Mountains, it cooled and condensed, dropping buckets of rain upon the high country. The highest official weather station was at Somerset in the southern Green Mountains, where 9.65" of rain was recorded, but rainfall was even heavier at higher elevations and some observers believe as much as 15" fell in this one storm.

This incredible rainfall would easily have been enough to cause flooding, but the situation was exacerbated by what had been a wetter-than-average October. Throughout the state, streams were already running full and soils were saturated. On top of this, in 1927 Vermont was still primarily cleared, agricultural land, and there were few trees to slow run-off as there are today. The worst flooding occurred in the Winooski River Valley. Montpelier reported a high-water mark of 16.5' and water was 12' deep on Main and State Streets! Damage and deaths were heavy in many other towns including Wolcott, Bennington, Troy, Waterbury and Bolton, which had 26 deaths.

No matter what you think about Vermont's weather, it is never boring. If you don't like what you see out the window today, just wait until tomorrow. It's likely to be different. Perhaps the weather is what makes Vermonters hard-working individualists; no one else could survive here.

ACID RAIN

Frozen deep in the Greenland icecap, stacked one upon the other like ancient tomes, are the climatic records of years gone by. For millenia, the snow and rain which has fallen here has accumulated in distinct, annual layers which today scientists can read and interpret. They tell not only of the weather, but also of the chemistry of the earth's atmosphere, and what they tell about the quality of our air and water today compared to yesterday is greatly disturbing.

Samples of the ancient frozen rain and snow were compared to the precipitation now falling on New England. They show that today New England receives rain 30 to 40 times more acidic than that which fell from the skies in preindustrial days. This "acid rain" forms when industrial smokestacks— primarily coal-fired electrical generators—dump millions of tons of sulfur and nitrogen oxides into the atmosphere. These combine with water in the atmosphere to form sulfuric and nitric acid that subsequently falls on plants, crops, soils and into our lakes and streams. In addition to these acids, other air pollutants are constantly spewed into the atmosphere, including toxic, heavy metals like lead, zinc, copper, vanadium and cadmium.

Natural rainwater is slightly acidic, with a pH measurement of about 5.6. Vermont's rain is usually set at 4.0 to 4.6. pH. The pH scale is a logarithmic scale— each whole number increment represents a tenfold change. Thus Vermont's precipitation is on the average at least 10 times more acidic than normal rainwater. The most acidic rainfall ever recorded in the state was 2.75 pH at West Dover, in 1980!

If you think Vermont's skies are not as blue as they used to be, you're right. Research conducted in the Burlington area showed that average visibility was reduced about 45 percent by sulfate air pollution. Since most of the air pollution entering Vermont is the product of power plant emissions in the Midwest, Vermonters are essentially subsidizing the electrical consumption of users outside the state—people who are not paying the real costs for what they receive.

Other research done at the University of Vermont by Doctors Volgelmann and Klein has documented declines in the high elevation forests of Camel's Hump and other mountains. Since 1965, they discovered, 50 percent of the red spruce on Camel's Hump has died. In addition,

Acid rain and heavy metals associated with air pollution are thought to be responsible for an unusually high death rate among spruce, sugar maples and other trees in Vermont's mountains.
GEORGE WUERTHNER

other species like sugar maple have experienced a sharp reduction in growth rate and seedling survival. The economic consequences of declining tree productivity could be disastrous for Vermont's forest-dependent industries, including its maple sugar production.

Although it was originally suspected that increasingly acidic precipitation was responsible for the losses, it is becoming clear that it is the synergism of acid rainfall and heavy metals which is the real culprit. Lead, for example, is toxic to many living organisms at very low levels. The chemical was found on the forest floor on Camel's Hump in concentrations equivalent to measurements made in urban areas of New Jersey!

The mountain forests are particularly vulnerable to the effects of polluted air for several reasons. Mountains usually receive greater amounts of rainfall than do the valleys because of orographic lift. Because there is more rain, there is more acid deposition. In addition, fog is common at higher elevations and is often twice as acidic as acid rain. Finally, as the mountains' winter snowpack melts, it releases all the acid precipitation accumulated over the previous winter in a sudden surge. The wave of acidity shocks tree roots and soil organisms living in the upper drainages of watersheds.

But air pollution is killing more than trees. Studies of the state's ponds and streams show increases in acidity which may soon be lethal to fish. In the Adirondacks to the west, fish losses due to lake acidification have already been documented. Those watersheds typified by granitic bedrock are especially vulnerable; thus the broad belt of waters lying atop granites on the east side of the Green Mountains and in the Northeast Kingdom are particularly endangered.

Finally, no one knows for certain what the long-term, cumulative impacts will be on human health. What happens when we are constantly breathing air loaded with sulfates, acids and toxic heavy metals? The simplest, and safest, guess is that it can't be good. Air pollution is just one problem among an increasing number that transcends state borders and is beyond the limited powers of Vermont's town governments, even at times those of its state government.

CHAPTER FIVE

HISTORICAL FOUNDATIONS

The first people to enter what would become the state of Vermont left no written record, but there is evidence of their passage. In the closing days of the last Ice Age, when the Champlain basin was an arm of the ocean, Paleo-Indians first ventured into the region. Perhaps as early as 9300 BC they were hunting herds of caribou and now-extinct big game species like the mastodon, which roamed the tundra-parklands that then dominated here. The Champlain Sea itself may have provided rich food resources such as seals, whales and possibly walrus.

The Paleo-Indian hunters were thought to have been so successful that within 2,000 years of their arrival in Vermont, they may have precipitated the extinction of some of the larger Ice Age mammals, already stressed by the changing environmental conditions. Shortly after humans first entered Vermont, a long-term climatic warming trend began, bringing about alterations in the vegetation and the Ice Age animals' habitats. More than 100 types of large mammals disappeared from North America, including most of the important prey species of the early human hunters. Big-game hunting culture thus came to an end and the area was abandoned.

From about 7000 BC until perhaps as late as 3000 BC, no people are thought to have lived in Vermont. There is considerable debate about this, however, as some claim a lack of archaeological evidence does not necessarily mean there was no one here. The climate became increasingly warm and dry, and by 3000 BC average temperatures were considerably hotter than they are today. Forests gradually evolved to something approaching our present mix of northern hardwoods and conifers, with eastern hemlock, white pine and red spruce.

Gradually humans moved back to the state (if indeed they ever had left) and their lifestyle reflected the changed environment. Although deer, bear and moose continued to be important parts of their diet, more emphasis was placed on gathering plant foods. This hunting-and-gathering culture survived for several thousand years and evidence exists in numerous sites in the Lake Champlain lowlands, the Connecticut River Valley and along Otter Creek.

The beginning of the modern Indian period was marked by some substantial innovations and changes in lifestyle which appeared among Midwestern peoples sometime between the years 1600 BC and 600 BC. These included cultivation of domestic crops, pottery-making and use of the bow and arrow. The new practices and technology slowly spread eastward. Vermont Indians probably did not acquire the bow and arrow until around 1000 AD, or approximately 100 years after the Vikings had colonized Greenland. The earliest indication of Indian agriculture in the state comes from corn cobs and kernels, and other debris found in a site along the Winooski River near Burlington that was occupied from 1470 to 1480 AD, or just 12 years before Christopher Columbus sailed into the Caribbean.

As in the earlier periods, most Indian habitation occurred along Lake Champlain, Otter Creek and occasionally the Connecticut River Valley. Not surprisingly, these are the same areas that are most densely populated today. Archaeological finds from other parts of the state are rare or nonexistent, a fact which led to the popular notion that Indians did not inhabit Vermont. And indeed, compared to the more benign and resource-rich regions of southern New England, Vermont had few residents— perhaps no more than several thousand people when the first Europeans arrived on the scene.

Delegates framed Vermont's constitution in this Windsor location during a July 1777 convention. Then-progressive ideas included the prohibition of slavery and universal sufferage for adult males.
GEORGE WUERTHNER

Facing page, left: DAVID M. STONE

Right: Old cedar fence on South Hero Island in Lake Champlain. Since the arrival of Paleo-Indian groups as early as 9300 BC, the Lake Champlain lowlands have been the most favorable location for human habitation in what would become Vermont. The region's attractiveness for settlement continues today, and the state's highest population density is found around the lake.
GEORGE WUERTHNER

Above: Vermont's famed stone could reach regional markets with the advent of rail and machine. This is probably at Barre, ca. 1895.
VERMONT HISTORICAL SOCIETY

Right: Inhabitants of the New Hampshire Grants, precursor of Vermont, first voted to seek independence from New York and New Hampshire at Dorset.

Facing page: Vermont sent 20 percent of its male population to fight in the Civil War—a higher percentage than any other state. Statues such as this one in Newfane are a common sight throughout Vermont. GEORGE WUERTHNER PHOTOS

Early European Explorers

When the first French explorers wandered into Vermont in the 1600s, the local Indians, the Abenaki, were living in several major villages along Lake Champlain and a few smaller, seasonally occupied sites in the Connecticut River valley. The Abenaki lived part of the year in fortress-like villages which protected them from attacking enemy tribes like the Iroquois. Nearby they grew crops that supplemented a wide variety of wild plants and fish and big game.

The first European to see the land we call Vermont was Samuel Champlain. In 1609, he traveled up the giant lake that now bears his name, in the company of two other Frenchmen and 60 Algonquin Indians. Near the site of the later Fort Ticonderoga, the Algonquins were engaged in a battle with their enemies the Iroquois. The Iroquois never forgave the French for aligning themselves with the Algonquins. This battle set the stage for future alliances in which the Iroquois sided with the British, while the Algonquins, which included Vermont's Abenakis, became backers of the French. For the next 150 years the French and British, along with their respective Indian allies, struggled for control of North America. The waterways of Vermont would serve as the bloody routes to battle for the warriors on all sides.

The French were also the first to build a permanent settlement in Vermont. In 1666, French soldiers constructed Fort Saint Anne on Isle La Motte, an island in the northern reaches of Lake Champlain. Attempting to control the strategic Champlain waterway, other French outposts soon followed at Crown Point and Ticonderoga. Meanwhile, Dutch and British settlers were moving into the region from the south. Fort Orange, a Dutch settlement on the Hudson River near present-day Albany, was built in 1624, while British colonists were setting up towns along the Massachusetts coast; Plymouth was settled in 1620 and Boston in 1630. Traders and settlers soon spread out from these communities and began to explore the mountains and valleys of New England, including those of the Green Mountain State.

These forts and towns served not only as military bases, but also as trading posts. French, Dutch and English traders obtained furs from the Indians in exchange for European goods, which included blankets, knives, axes and guns. The fur trade intensified conflicts between tribes as each group sought to control trapping territories. The pressure from the Iroquois forced the Abenaki to abandon some of their outlying villages and collect into their larger settlements, which were fortified with log ramparts.

Intermingling with these tribal conflicts then, the struggle between the two great European powers— France and Britain— spilled over the Atlantic onto the eastern edge of North America. In 1664 the Dutch surrendered all of their North American colonies to the British, giving them control of the eastern seaboard south of New France. With the withdrawal of the Dutch as a contender for the New World territories, the fighting between French and British carried on for more than 100 years. It finally culminated in the French and Indian War, but the North American conflict was merely one theater in the last round of war between the two great adversaries. The French eventually conceded defeat in 1763, signing the Treaty of Paris, which, among other things ended French control of Vermont.

The British and the Rebels

The British wasted no time in seizing their opportunity. The colony of New Hampshire was established in 1741, and new governor Benning Wentworth claimed that New Hampshire's western boundary followed a north-south line 20 miles east of the Hudson River, as was the case for the borders of Connecticut and Massachusetts. Wentworth's admittedly brash interpretation of boundary lines brought him into sharp conflict with the colony of New York, which argued that it had been granted the disputed territory under a 1664 charter. Ignoring New York's protests, Governor Wentworth began to grant his own charters for towns within the "New Hampshire Grants."

The first town in the new territory was Bennington, which Wentworth had humbly named for himself. It stood on the Walloomsac River, some 40 miles west of the Connecticut River and well within the area claimed by New York. New York's governor objected to Wentworth's actions, but to no avail— as Wentworth blithely continued to charter new townships. By 1764 he had established 138 towns covering 3 million acres, which he had given or sold to relatives, associates and high government officials. Wentworth judiciously retained 65,000 acres for himself. After the conclusion of the French and Indian War in 1763, British settlers began to pour into Vermont, buying up the parcels that Wentworth earlier had doled out.

Not to be outdone, New York's governor also was granting town charters in the same region, many of which overlapped with Wentworth's grants. Conflicts between settlers increased as people discovered the dubious nature of their property deeds. To settle the question of who had legal authority in the contested area,

Above: By 1830 all the land that could be tilled was in agricultural production, and Vermont's population stabilized. Many sons and daughters were forced to leave the state to find tillable lands of their own, or other employment.
VERMONT HISTORICAL SOCIETY

Facing page, top: Logging the state's white pines and other trees was a major industry in the 1800s. At one time or another, nearly all the state's forests were logged or cleared so that virgin old-growth trees are non-existent.
VERMONT HISTORICAL SOCIETY

Bottom: The coming of the railroads had a major impact upon Vermont's economy, enabling products from milk to granite memorials to be shipped to out-of-state markets.
PHILIP KEENAN

both Wentworth and New York's Governor Clinton agreed to present their arguments to the British king, who ruled in favor of New York. New York then requested that all settlers on the New Hampshire Grant lands pay a fee to New York in order to retain title to land, which of course they believed they already had purchased legally. The infuriated New Hampshire grantees petitioned the king for relief. In 1767, the king instructed New York officials to refrain from molesting the region's settlers and to abstain from issuing any more charters there.

Despite the king's order, New York continued to issue titles to lands that overlapped the New Hampshire Grants. The conflicts between "Yorkers" and the Grants settlers intensified. In 1770, Yorker grantees attempted to remove nine Wentworth settlers from their land in the Bennington area by filing ejection suits in a New York court at Albany. The Hampshire Grant settlers felt that if the Yorker officials were successful in removing the "Bennington Nine," as they were known, the validity of their own lands would be jeopardized. A defense for the nine was organized and a young, fast-talking man named Ethan Allen was elected to coordinate the legal efforts. Allen obtained documents supporting the legitimacy of the Hampshire Grants, but the New York chief justice (who himself owned titles to New York grants overlapping New Hampshire Grants) refused to accept the New Hampshire documents as evidence. Allen

concluded that a fair trial could not take place in New York, so rode to Bennington where he established the "Green Mountain Boys," who would protect the Hampshire land titles by force, if need be. The Yorkers disdainfully referred to Allen's group as the "Bennington Mob."

Mob or not, the New Yorkers underestimated the resolve of the people of the New Hampshire Grants. The Green Mountain Boys announced that no New York surveyors would be allowed in the territory, nor would they tolerate titles from New York. In 1771, Allen and his Boys made good their proclamation, driving Yorker settlers from lands near Poultney and Rupert and turning back a New York surveyor and sheriff who had entered onto the Grants. In November, the New York governor and council declared Allen and his comrades outlaws, and issued rewards for their capture. When the flamboyant Ethan heard of the decision, he responded in kind by offering a reward for the capture of key New York officials.

During a 1774 convention in Manchester, the Grantees further separated themselves from New York by passing a resolution that forbade all inhabitants of the region to hold any political office under New York authority, and declared all New Yorkers public enemies. In 1775, a New York sheriff attempted to enforce foreclosure proceedings on farmers in Westminster, along the Connecticut River. An unruly crowd gathered to protest the action and the sheriff and his deputies ended up killing one man and wounding another. This incident became known as the "Westminster Massacre," and helped unify Hampshire Grantees on both sides of the territory against New York authority.

Despite the Green Mountain Boys' reputation as an outlaw band, they joined forces in 1775 with Benedict Arnold and a Connecticut regiment to capture the British-held Fort Ticonderoga. This action, along with the Battle of Lexington and Concord the month before, signaled the beginnings of the American Revolution.

American Independence

At the same time that the American colonies were preparing for their independence from Britain, the Hampshire Grants was the site of a series of conventions in 1776 and 1777, in which resolutions were passed to organize a new and independent state that eventually would be called Vermont. The Vermont constitutional delegates fully expected their state to be accepted into the Union with the other 13 colonies, but its admittance was blocked— primarily by New York, which maintained that it still held jurisdiction over the area. Thus rebuffed by the Continental Congress, Vermont was an independent republic for 14 years, issuing its own money, establishing a postal service and raising its own troops until it was finally admitted to the Union as the 14th state in 1791.

When its admission into the new nation was temporarily blocked, some Vermont officials entered into negotiations with the British in Quebec. They discussed a possible merger with British Canada. The Allen brothers led these secret talks, and bargained for provincial status and legal recognition of their vast land holdings along Lake Champlain. They threatened the Continental Congress with a Vermont-Canada alliance as a ploy to force the granting of statehood.

The idea that Vermont might defect and become a British ally prompted some members of Congress to call for a military invasion of the republic, but the American colonies already were overextended in their battle for independence from Great Britain. Taking on another war was beyond their means. Realizing that its existence was precarious at best, Vermont eventually agreed to pay $30,000 to New York as compensation for the loss of the disputed territory, and so cleared the path for its admittance into the United States in 1791.

With the legal status of its lands cleared, Yankee settlers were soon streaming into the state. Its population grew from 85,000 in 1791 when it joined the Union, to 154,000 by 1800, and 217,000 by 1810.

In clearing trees for cultivation and habitation, Vermont's settlers produced the first export items— timber and potash. The latter material was used in the manufacture of soap and glass. The new farms soon were producing an excess of crops like wheat, buckwheat, barley and oats. These grains were used for human and, just as important, horse consumption.

In 1811, merino sheep were brought to the state, initiating a boom in wool production and soon taking Vermont to the lead position in wool production in the country. With the growth of the sheep herds came the development of manufacturing as mills began to process the wool and weave the yarn into cloth. Bennington, Colchester, Middlebury and Springfield became the state's foremost textile centers. Thousands of acres of forest were cleared to make new pasture, to satisfy the increasing demand for wool. By 1840, some 1.7 million sheep grazed Vermont's hillsides.

By the 1830s, nearly all of the state's potential farmland had been in agricultural production. It also was rapidly declining in productivity due to soil erosion and poor farming methods. The deluge of settlers to

Vermont slowed to a trickle and many of the state's young people began to move off the worn-out farms and onto the western frontier. By 1850 an estimated 145,000 people born in Vermont were living outside of the state. Vermont slipped into an economic and social hibernation that would last for more than a hundred years.

The onset of economic hard times seems to have made Vermonters receptive to religious conversion. During the early years of settlement, many pioneers had apparently left behind their devotion to worship and some, such as Ethan Allen, vehemently attacked established religious doctrine. To the clergy of southern New England, Vermont was ruled by a faithless, drunken rabble that desperately needed to hear the word of God. A major evangelical campaign was mounted by Congregationalists and Presbyterians to enlighten Vermont's "heathenish hordes." Revivals were held throughout Vermont and the ranks of Baptist, Congregational and other Protestant churches swelled. Today these same denominations still dominate the state.

As new religious sects enlivened Vermont's spiritual realms, the railroads helped bring new vitality to the state's economy. They first arrived in Vermont in 1849 and 1850; the impact was profound. Previously, the state's geography, characterized by uneven, rough terrain and the absence of a seaport, prevented Vermonters from readily exploiting distant markets. Exports had to

51

IRA & ETHAN ALLEN

No two men influenced Vermont's early history more than the legendary Allen brothers, Ethan and Ira. They were bold, irreverent and a little rough around the edges. They were political gamblers, not diplomats; rabble rousers, not statesmen. They were motivated by more than mild self-interest—some say—to assure the independence of the state. Ethan was the eldest of six brothers, and perhaps the most colorful and outrageous. He is also the best known. Depending on one's perspective, Ethan was a swaggering hero, or an impious opportunist and manipulator. There is no doubt that he was extremely cocky, even arrogant, and that he enjoyed drinking, spirited debate and thumbing his nose at authority— be it the New York legislature or organized religion.

In 1771, Ethan left Connecticut for the territory then known as the New Hampshire Grants, and with his brothers founded the Onion River Land Company. The Allens bought thousands of acres along Lake Champlain and the Winooski River, hoping to cash in on the land hunger of new settlers. The success of their plans depended on secure title to their properties, and more than one historian has speculated that Ethan's later military and political involvement sprang more from a desire to retain ownership of his holdings than from a sense of patriotism.

Ethan first rose to prominence after his appearance in 1770 in a New York court, where he defended the legality of the New Hampshire grants. When the Yorkers suggested that the grantees' resistance was useless, Allen is reported to have answered: "The gods of the valleys are not the gods of the hills!" He returned to Vermont and organized the Green Mountain Boys, who successfully kept the New York authorities out of the disputed region. For this and other deeds, the New York Assembly created a bounty for Ethan's capture, dead or alive. The indomitable Allen responded characteristically. He declared New York officials outlaws and offered a reward, in turn, for their apprehension.

Fort Ticonderoga was Ethan's prize in 1775, when he, the Green Mountain Boys and the support forces of Benedict Arnold and some Massachusetts militiamen, captured the strategic post from the British. Later, upon learning that Montreal was poorly defended, Ethan brashly tried to storm the city, but was captured and spent two and a half years of the Revolutionary War in an English prison. Released in 1779, he returned to Vermont and became a representative in the American Congress and later in the State Assembly.

He was arraigned in 1782 by the Vermont Legislature for his participation in the Haldimand Negotiations. These secret talks between the British and several prominent Vermont citizens, including Ethan and his brother Ira, concerned the possible annexation of Vermont to English-controlled Quebec. The Allens maintained that this was merely a diplomatic ploy, to nudge the Continental Congress towards acceptance of Vermont into the Union. But others charged that the brothers were primarily interested in securing their own land claims, and cared little which flag eventually flew over the Green Mountains. Ethan, dismayed that the state he had fought to bring into existence could later doubt his motives, retreated from politics to live out his life on his farm near Burlington.

After his retirement from active politics, Ethan wrote Reason—Man's Only Oracle, which was published in 1785 and blasted the established religious doctrine of the day. Vindictive clergy pronounced that God had fittingly answered Ethan's blasphemy when the heathenous rebel passed out in a drunken stupor and froze to death one cold winter night in 1789. Despite his

Ethan Allen's homestead along the Winooski River near Burlington.
GEORGE WUERTHNER

less-than-glorious demise, Ethan was buried with full military honors in Green Mount Cemetery in Burlington.

Ira Allen, though less flamboyant than his brother, was at one time one of the wealthiest men in America. Yet he died a pauper in Philadelphia and lies there in an unmarked grave. He began his career in Vermont in 1771, and dabbled for a time in land surveying. Joining his brother in opposition of British and New York rule, he devised a plan to confiscate the properties of British sympathizers. The money obtained from their sale went toward outfitting a Vermont regiment. Of course, ever the patriot, Ira had been one of the anxious buyers.

Ira Allen was an author of the state constitution and he composed its preamble. He subsequently was elected the state's first treasurer and Surveyor-General. By both legal and not-so-legal means, he soon owned vast tracts of Vermont land and was one of the state's richest citizens. As a wedding gift, he gave his bride the deed to Irasburg in 1789. He also granted land and money to the state to begin the University of Vermont.

As a result of the Haldimand Negotiations, Ira's loyalty and honesty were called into question. He lost his state offices; an economic depression sent land prices tumbling and Ira was beset by debt and creditors. He journeyed to Europe, where he secured a loan and purchased rifles which he hoped to sell for a profit in the U.S. His ship was stopped by the British, who found the arms and accused him of aiding Irish rebels. The unlucky entrepreneur spent the next five years in a British jail before he could clear his name.

By the time Ira returned to Vermont, his land had been sold for taxes. The British finally released his rifles, but the money from their sale promptly went to Ira's creditors. The destitute Allen was put in prison. He managed at last to raise the bail for his release and fled the state. In 1814, he died penniless in Philadelphia.

be fairly light, easily handled and non-perishable. By the same token, imports that did not meet these criteria came very dear.

Railroads Brought Change

On the railroads Vermont farmers could ship their products to far-away urban markets in Boston and New York. The dairy industry came into its own as perishable foods like butter, cheese and milk could be carried rapidly to large population centers.

Another industry that flourished in the wake of the new railways was quarrying great blocks of marble, granite and slate, which formerly had been prohibitively expensive to ship out of state. Vermont soon was a leader in the production of these materials.

Timber, too, was developing as a major export item. In 1840, there were more than a thousand lumber mills in the state and when the rails reached Vermont, logging truly took off. The railroads also were able to reach the trees that previously had been left uncut because they were too far from a usable waterway. Before train transportation became available, timber was moved in great log drives down the state's rivers. But with the coming of the railways, loggers could lay temporary tracks up into the hills and access the most remote timber stands. Even the high-elevation spruce and fir forests were not exempt from the lumberjack's axe.

The trains not only moved wood, they also consumed it. In 1874 it was estimated that 500,000 cords of wood were burned in Vermont engines annually, further depleting state's timber resources.

Not only were Vermont's natural resources opened up to new exploitation, the manufacturing industry also was able to develop— even flourish— with the state's connections to outside markets. The growth of the machine-tool or "precision" industry, centered in Springfield and Windsor on the Connecticut River, came about largely because of the rapid transport provided by the rails.

The railroads carried more than raw materials and finished goods in and out of the state, but, of course, moved people as well. Vermont's tourist trade had its earliest beginnings in the late 1800s, when mountaintop and mineral springs resorts attracted wealthy city dwellers from Boston and New York City.

And if people could come to Vermont on the rails, they also could leave. They did, in droves. With 314,000 residents in 1850, the state's population hardly had changed by 1900, when there were 342,000 inhabitants. One reason for this excruciatingly slow growth was that

thousands of Vermont-born youth kept moving out, seeking better economic opportunities elsewhere.

When the Civil War broke out in 1861, the same rails shipped Vermont men and boys south to fight. Vermont sent a higher fraction (20 percent) of its male citizenry to the war than any other state in the union and 13,695 of them died during the four-year struggle. Today, Civil War monuments are a common fixture of Vermont's village greens.

Despite the growth of manufacturing, even as late as 1920 Vermont's non-agricultural population still constituted only 10 percent of the work force. Dairy farming remained the single most common occupation through the early 20th century; Vermont continued to be the most rural state in the nation. With a less than one percent growth rate between 1910 and 1940, there was scarcely any new blood to challenge the state's long-standing political structure. The foundation of that structure is best summarized by the maxim, "the least government is the best government."

20th Century Leaders

President Calvin Coolidge, born in Plymouth and succeeding to the presidency in 1923 after the death of Warren Harding, exemplified this spartan attitude towards government. "Silent Cal" was known for his pinched speech as well as his restrained political style, which critics referred to as the "caretaker approach."

Top: Birthplace of President Calvin Coolidge at Plymouth. After his death at age 61, he was buried in the family plot in his hometown.

Bottom: Dairying became the major agricultural enterprise after railroad access made it possible to market fresh milk to population centers like Boston and New York. Dairy farming became the most common occupation during the late 1800s and early 1900s. GEORGE WUERTHNER PHOTOS

53

One famous Coolidge quote is: "The business of America is business." When Silent Cal decided not to seek re-election in 1928, he made his intentions known in a characteristically direct and undecorated statement: "I do not choose to run for President in 1928." That was all he needed to say.

Despite the popular appeal of Coolidge's "less is best" philosophy, Vermont experienced a profound shift in its social, economic and political traditions in the late 1920s. It was precipitated, literally, in November 1927 when rain poured down on the Green Mountain State for three days and left more than a foot of water over much of the state. Eighty five people died, entire herds of cattle were lost, thousands of acres of agricultural land were laid to waste, and the state's transportation network was in a shambles. Faced with a monumental rebuilding task, Governor John Weeks convened a special session of the legislature and requested $8 million for reconstruction of bridges, roads and other public works. Until this time, most of the responsibility for administering public services had been held by the local Boards of Selectmen, but the 1927 Flood was so devastating that recovery was possible only through state assistance and coordination. This resulted in a major shift of power to the state level. In 1931, an income tax was initiated to fund the new demands placed on the state. In addition, until the 1927 Flood Vermont had steadfastly refused federal aid, but during this reconstruction era, it asked for and received some $2.5 million to help repair the flood damage. New dams for flood control also were constructed at federal expense.

Through the 1930s the federal government increasingly provided the public and social services the state's small population could not fund for itself. The state willingly accepted the aid, but all the while continued to declare its independence of outside authority. Vermont was one of the few states that did not support President Franklin Roosevelt's New Deal policies, yet the Civilian Conservation Corps program alone employed more than 40,000 men in the state.

In 1936, George Aiken was one of only four Republican governors to be elected in the country. Aiken was renowned for his unrelenting attacks on the New Deal, yet like his predecessor John Weeks, he willingly accepted federal money and benefits. Ironically, Aiken went on to become a U.S. Senator for 36 years and was one of the chief architects of the federal Food Stamp program. It was something Roosevelt would have admired.

Above: The town of Irasburg, bought by Ira Allen and given to his wife as a wedding present, is one of many place names that now commemorate the Allen brothers in Vermont.
GEORGE WUERTHNER

Right: George Aiken, a native of Putney, was Governor of Vermont and later served for 36 years in the U.S. Senate. Aiken was known for his modest style. He didn't feel comfortable in Washington's social whirl and advised that, when visiting the White House, one should "get a seat near the door so when they dim the lights, you can sneak out."
VERMONT HISTORICAL SOCIETY

TOWNS

Members of the 251 Club have an unusual hobby. They collect towns. More precisely, they "collect" visits to Vermont's 246 towns (and the five that are not legally organized) and its eight cities. The complete collection, which belongs to "plus" members who have seen all Green Mountain State civic units, embraces everything from "Queen City" Burlington, population 37,840, to rather lonely Lewis, an unorganized town in the northeast corner that has never known one permanent resident. For all the present-day differences among Vermont communities, however, the towns share one very important, and uncommon, feature: a strong local government with a level of autonomy that is almost unmatched by municipalities in other states.

The town as a unit of government was born early in the colonial period. In New England, as separate communities began to multiply on the fringes of the original settlements, they were granted the ability to determine local issues and set local laws for themselves. The town citizens (all land-owning men) gathered regularly to discuss and vote on issues. Eventually, committees of "selectmen" were elected to tend to town matters between meetings, which occurred at increasingly distant intervals.

When settlers moved from southern New England into the "new frontier" of Vermont, they instituted a similar style of municipal management. The town meeting, eventually an annual event, became the fountainhead of local governance, where policy is formulated, where officers are elected, where tax rates are set and ordinances passed. The town, locally and independently controlled, has been an enduring, peculiarly apt form of government for the Green Mountain State. The terrain is broken and uneven, keeping people clustered in villages and the villages somewhat isolated from one another. Most towns were small, and still are. In the first two centuries of white occupation, Vermont was dominantly agrarian. The citizenry depended on the locality to provide basic needs and sustain the economy; thus they had a great deal of interest in what happened to the land and community they depended on. Of course, the conditions during the creation and shaping of the New England states and their form of local government changed with time and the expansion of America. Besides Vermont, 16 other states (settled largely by New Englanders) employ the town as a legally-recognized civic unit. In the rest of the nation, the county is the basic structure of local control. However, in no place except New England are towns very active or important. And only in New England is the local governmental unit actually self-legislating. Counties usually have few, if any, local laws, and county officials act essentially as arms of the state government, administering state laws. As urbanization and concomitant suburbanization have crept over southern New England, towns there also have lost their influence, so that it may well be said that only in Vermont and perhaps parts of northern New Hampshire and Maine, towns still are viable, functioning polities.

Today the agrarian, locally-focused way of life that gave birth to and sustained the New England town is disappearing even in Vermont. Skeptics preach the demise of the town, claiming that in an era of increasingly strong state and federal government, where improved transportation and communication have drastically cut the distance and time from one town to another autonomy is an illusion and an impossibility. Even the venerated Town Meeting—say critics—has become a farce.

Once a greatly anticipated rite of spring, Town Meeting Day on the first Tuesday of March now is ignored or forgotten by a majority of Vermonters. Today in many places the selectmen and other town officers are elected, and the town budget is voted on by secret ballot on Town Meeting Day; the open floor meeting is held the night before and offers few significant issues for consideration. The inevitable result, some observers say, is poor attendance.

The Annual Report, too, presents a juicy encyclopedia of town statistics and the laboriously itemized—and tediously scrutinized—selectmen's proposed budget. But while townspeople relish lists of the past year's marriages, births, deaths and tax delinquencies, the really hard numbers—the

Waits River. JEFF GNASS

rising amount of state and federal monies put into the municipal coffers, the multiplying second home and resort developments, the accelerating influx of new residents and the swelling school rolls—these are not discussed. And even if they were, towns do not have the sovereignty or the expertise to fully grapple with these complex, state- and region-wide problems.

Will the Town Meeting be put aside for a "more practical" process of local democracy? Is it fated to remain only as some public, psychological salve—satisfying an old Yankee itching to make laws (and a little trouble) every Mud Season or so?

One thing is certain. Vermont towns have many defenders, including many newcomers. They won't go down without a fight. And with what seems to be a nation-wide renaissance of interest in grassroots activism and local involvement, it may well be that the 251 Green Mountain State towns and cities will remain both various in character, and politically distinct.

CHAPTER SIX

LAKE CHAMPLAIN LOWLANDS

56

The counties of Vermont's northwest corner—Grand Isle, Franklin, Addison and Chittenden—comprise a region called the Lake Champlain Lowlands. Here, the terrain is characteristically level or modestly undulating; many large farms and the wide-open waters of Champlain lend a feeling of spaciousness to the landscape. The rivers winding down to the lake are broad and easygoing.

The steep west slope of the Green Mountains graces the eastern rim of the Champlain basin, so that from an elevation of 95' on the lakeshore, the region eventually rises to just above 4,000' on the summit of Mt. Mansfield, the highest point in the state. The alliance of lake, broad lowland and looming mountain slopes endows this part of Vermont with some of the most sublime vistas in the state.

Glaciers left their mark here, as they did in the rest of Vermont. The smoothed and polished outcrops of Grand Isle and Franklin counties are characteristic glacial features, as is the Lake Champlain basin itself, which was scoured by the advancing ice sheet. At various times during the Ice Age, the lowlands were inundated with water, not ice, and the sediments that settled out of these extensive glacial lakes are now rich, arable soils.

Ten thousand years after the continental ice disappeared, another force is creeping over and reshaping the landscape. It is known as urban sprawl, and it emanates not from the far north but from Vermont's (only) major metropolitan area—the "Queen City" of Burlington and its surrounding suburbs. Beyond greater Burlington there are several secondary trade centers, including St. Albans and Middlebury. Despite the region's relatively heavy urbanization, it also has a greater percentage of agricultural land than any other region of the state.

While the southern end of the Green Mountains is both broad and unbroken—a substantial impediment to east-west travel—the relatively narrow band of ridges bordering the Champlain Lowlands is cleft completely through at several points. The three low water gaps, carved by the Winooski, the Lamoille and the Missisquoi rivers, provide convenient east-west travel corridors. In addition to these important waterways, Otter Creek—the longest river flowing wholly within the state's borders—

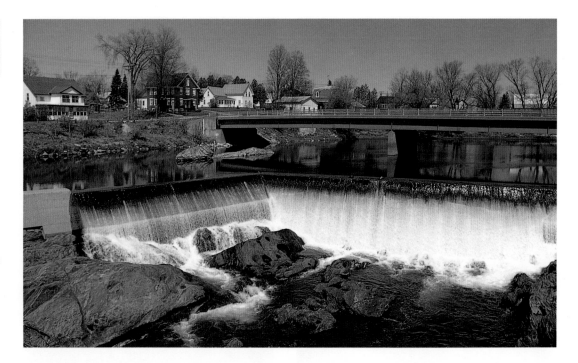

traces a northwest course through the region before emptying into Lake Champlain by Ferrisburg. Many communities, such as Middlebury, Vergennes, Enosburg Falls, Burlington and Swanton were sited on these streams because of the waterpower to operate grist mills and sawmills.

Large deltas fan out at the mouths of the rivers, where they empty into the quiet waters of Lake Champlain. One of the best developed "bird-foot" deltas in the country, so-called because from above they look like the splayed, webbed appendages of water fowl, is found at the terminus of the Missisquoi River near Swanton. This winding woodland of swamp and marsh is now protected wildlife habitat—officially the 5,839-acre Missisquoi National Wildlife Refuge, Vermont's only such federal sanctuary. The Missisquoi delta is an important staging and resting ground for migratory waterfowl, as well as nesting habitat for other birds such as great blue heron.

Algonquin and Iroquois

The wildlife-rich Champlain shore also once sustained a small population of Indians. They used the lake as a travel route for both trade and war. When the first

Waterfalls at Enosburg Falls.
GEORGE WUERTHNER

Facing page, left: Mallard ducks on a misty morning.
© NIELSEN PHOTO, FROM IMAGERY

Right: Looking across the Lake Champlain Lowlands toward the Adirondack Mountains of New York.
SONJA BULLATY

Above: Statue of Frenchman Samuel Champlain and Algonquin Indian guide at Fort St. Anne Shrine on Isla La Motte commemorates Champlain's explorations around the lake that bears his name. The site of the French-built fort constructed in 1666 was the first white settlement in what would become the state of Vermont.

Right: Winter sunset glow on Mt. Mansfield seen from Pleasant Valley.
GEORGE WUERTHNER PHOTOS

European to explore the region, the French Samuel de Champlain, paddled its length in 1609, several large, fortress-like Abenaki Indian villages stood along the Missisquoi and other rivers that emptied into the lake.

The Abenakis were a sub-group of the Algonquin Indians of Canada, and thus were enemies of the Mohawks and other Iroquois tribes that dominated New York. Even before European exploration, these tribes long had been at war. Upon commencement of the fur trade, in which the Indians swapped pelts for French, British and Dutch goods, the native groups vied for control of the fur-rich regions and between 1630 and 1760 the pitched battles—often joined by the European allies for both sides—made the Champlain region a bloody no-man's-land.

The constant threat of marauding war parties dampened British settlement of Vermont for many decades. Nevertheless, the French feared a British invasion and constructed a series of forts along Lake Champlain and its outlet, protecting their southern flank. The first European settlement built in Vermont, Fort St. Anne on Isle La Motte, was built by the French in 1666 as part of this defense system. The Lake Champlain region became an important theater of war in the world-wide, nearly 100-year conflict between the French and the English. The concluding chapter of the struggle in North America is known as the French and Indian War.

Lake Champlain in History

In this age of supersonic travel and nearly instant communication, it is difficult to imagine the incredible strategic importance Lake Champlain held for much of its human history. The waterway connected the St. Lawrence River and the lower Hudson Valley and, as the Indians knew long before the arrival of the Europeans, whoever controlled Champlain could also rule much of southern Canada and New England. For more than 200 years the French, English and eventually the Americans vied for dominion of this crucial corridor, building— and later grappling for control of— forts at Ticonderoga, Crown Point, and Chimney Point.

The French were the first to dominate the region. By the 1730s there were more than a thousand French settlers and soldiers living along Lake Champlain at Crown Point, Chimney Point and on the Alburg Peninsula. But during the closing days of the French and Indian War, the pioneers were forced back northward to Montreal to escape hostile forces. When the war ended in 1760 the British were in control of Lake Champlain and its military installations.

As it had been during the French and Indian War, Lake Champlain was of critical strategic importance during the American Revolution. In 1775, shortly after the Battle of Lexington, Ethan Allen and the Green Mountain Boys, along with Benedict Arnold and some militiamen, attacked the British garrison at Ticonderoga. The fort was taken by surprise and the rebel troops were able to capture it without resistance. Meanwhile, another contingent of the Green Mountain Boys under the command of Seth Warner easily took Crown Point, ensuring American control of the Champlain region.

In 1776, a large British force set sail from Canada and headed down Lake Champlain, intending to capture Albany, New York. Benedict Arnold and his small force of men hastily constructed several boats at the mouth of Otter Creek and sailed north to engage the much-larger British fleet. Arnold's boats surprised the British at Valcour Island, near South Hero Island, and a fierce battle ensued. The American flotilla slipped away during the night, but the English caught up with them and forced Arnold to scuttle his boats near the point from which they had been earlier launched. The British promptly captured Crown Point, but their invasion to the south was blunted. (In 1936, one of the boats lost by Arnold in the Valcour Island Battle was raised from the lake bottom and now is on display in the Smithsonian Institution in Washington, D.C.)

The following year, 1777, the British mounted a massive attack on Ticonderoga, capturing the fort and moving southward to take Albany. The British advance was halted by the Battle of Bennington,

After peace was reached with the British in 1783, settlement of the Champlain Lowlands began in earnest. One of the more desirable locations was along the Winooski, or Onion River as it then was called. Most of this land was owned by the Allen brothers' Onion River Land

Above: Limestone walls remain at Crown Point on the New York side of the lake opposite Vermont's Chimney Point. Crown Point was first occupied by the French, who constructed Saint Frederic in 1731. The British captured the site in 1759 and renamed it Crown Point. The fort, overlooking a narrows of the lake, controlled water travel between the Hudson River drainage to the south and the St. Lawrence River drainage to the north.

Left: The low islands in Grand Isle County are outcroppings of limestone built up in ancient tropical seas. The French first settled on Isle La Motte in the 1600s and quarried limestone. Many of the island's buildings such as the public library at Isle La Motte are built of this local stone. GEORGE WUERTHNER PHOTOS

A Farming Country

Farming dominated the early economy, although the clearing of the forests also produced potash and timber, both of which were exported to Canada via Lake Champlain. Shelburne became renowned for ship building, while Burlington grew into a major shipping center from which goods were sent north to Canada. In 1807, just prior to the War of 1812, President Jefferson pushed the Embargo Act through Congress. It prohibited trade with Britain and its Canadian territories. This was a severe blow to the settlers in northern Vermont who depended on the economic exchange with Canada. The Embargo Act split Vermonters on the issue of war with Britain and some openly suggested that the state consider joining Canada, rather than be economically destroyed. Many Vermonters ignored the embargo and smuggling was widely accepted. It was said that more than two thirds of the beef eaten by the British Canadian forces during the War of 1812 came from American farmers.

After this period of armed conflict, the region settled in for a long period of slow growth and development. The lake became Vermont's inland "seaway" as shipping and commerce came to dominate towns such as Burlington. As early as 1808, steamboats were floating across the lake waters. In 1823 the Champlain Canal linked the lake with the Hudson River and so made southern markets more accessible to Vermonters, and boosted the commercial importance of the region.

The advent of the railroads shifted some economic power away from Burlington, which was on a siding track of the main road that passed through Essex Junction and continued north to Montreal. St. Albans assumed a new importance as its railroad depot became the largest in New England.

The railroads made it possible for local farmers to ship perishable products like milk to outside markets. This marked the beginning of dairying as the major agricultural enterprise of the region. It also gave impetus to other export industries, including marble quarrying at Middlebury, textile manufacturing at Middlebury and Colchester and lumber-milling at Burlington.

During the Civil War the rails facilitated transport of Vermont troops to the southern fronts. George Stannard of St. Albans, who became a colonel of Vermont's Fourth Regiment of Militia, was the first person to volunteer his service to the Union cause. Although northern soil saw little action, the Green Mountain State boasted one small incident. Twenty-two Confederate soldiers raided two St. Albans banks and fled across the Canadi-

Above: The Lake Champlain Lowlands have the highest concentration of cleared agricultural land in the state. Four of five of the state's Class 1 agricultural counties are located here. GEORGE WUERTHNER

Facing page, top: Summer sunset over Lake Champlain. IMAGERY
Bottom: Lake Champlain is served by ferries that connect towns on the New York and Vermont sides.
GEORGE WUERTHNER

Company, including portions of Burlington, Colchester and Jericho.

The Allens actively promoted settlement and, unlike most real-estate speculators, actually lived on the lands they were trying to sell. Ira Allen built a water-powered mill in 1772 on the falls of the Winooski River to grind grain and saw lumber. He also constructed a stockade, named Fort Frederick, for protection against Indian raids. With the nearby lake for transportation, an abundance of good fertile farmland and the rudimentary beginnings of a town already established, the Allens had no trouble attracting new settlers to their towns once the Revolutionary War ended. Rapid growth continued and by 1800 there were 9,395 people in Chittenden County; by 1810 the population had reached 14,646 and the Lake Champlain Lowlands had established itself as the state's most populous region—a distinction it still has today.

an border with $208,000. They later were captured in Montreal and tried in Canada, but acquitted on the grounds that the raid was an "act of war." The hold-up was a Confederate diversionary measure, attempted in hopes that Union troops would consequently be stationed along the northern border, and thus kept from participation in military action to the south.

Through the late 1800s, this region attracted limited numbers of immigrants, particularly from Quebec. The French-Canadians came to work in the woolen and cotton mills that lined the Winooski River near Burlington; others sought jobs on farms or on logging operations. French-Canadians still migrate to Vermont's northern tier, but many more simply come to sight-see and find recreation in the Green Mountains. The great population center of metropolitan Montreal, less than 70 miles to the north, guarantees a ready source of relaxation-seeking urban dwellers.

Despite the influx of immigrants, the Champlain Lowlands actually saw little population growth from 1860 through the 1950s. In all of Vermont, two residents left the state for every newcomer. The economy was relatively stagnant, though a few industries such as lumbering, and textiles brought limited prosperity. Farming continued to dominate the hinterlands.

Towns of Today

Around 1960, all this changed as the region underwent an economic surge, particularly in Chittenden County. The growth continues today as new industry and people discover the region's high quality of life. With Burlington as the fountainhead of development and burgeoning economic activity, the waves have reached beyond the immediate boundaries of the city to the surrounding towns. St. Albans, for example, has the second highest yearly growth rate, at 7 percent, in the state. Although this expansion of human presence and activity poses an unavoidable challenge to the environment and traditional ways of life, at least almost all the growth thus far has been associated with light, relatively clean, high-tech industries and the services that support them.

The main focus of change is, of course, the city of Burlington. The surrounding towns are economically dependent on this urban center, and function increasingly as bedroom communities for commuting workers. In fact, the Greater Burlington area labor force now accounts for 32 percent of Vermont's employed people. In 1986, an estimated 122,000 people lived in Chittenden County— predominantly in or next to Burlington. The Queen City itself had 37,727 residents (1980 figures),

Above: Middlebury College, founded in 1800, whose buildings are constructed of local stone, has one of the most elegant campuses in the nation. GEORGE WUERTHNER

Right: Cultural events are common in the Lake Champlain region. Here, concert goers at the Mozart Festival have dinner. JOHN LYNCH

Top: The Central Vermont Railroad was a major economic force in St. Albans, a town now experiencing a revitalization as businesses relocate here. The town has the distinction of being the site of the only Civil War action to occur in Vermont. In 1864, 22 Confederate soldiers raided three St. Albans banks. GEORGE WUERTHNER

while Colchester had 12,629, Winooski 6,318, Essex Junction 7,032, Essex Town 14,392, and South Burlington 10,697. The smaller towns like Underhill (2,172), Jericho (3,575) and Shelburne (5,000) are also largely commuter residences.

In fact, downtown Burlington— with its new high-rise office buildings, malls and highway strips— hardly fits at all one's image of rural, quiet Vermont. For several miles on the highway between Burlington and Shelburne, for example, hardly an empty lot is left among the fast-food restaurants, supermarkets and car dealerships. The remarkable panoramic view of the Adirondack Mountains across Lake Champlain, once a highlight of this stretch of road, now is glimpsed only through take-out driveways and over parking lots.

Outside of the Burlington area, there are just a few significant population centers. St. Albans, to the north, is the largest community in Franklin County with ap-

proximately 13,000 people. The major employers include Fonda Paper and Container, Ever Ready Battery, St. Albans Co-op Creamery, and Central Vermont Railroad.

Vergennes, with 2,300 citizens, has the distinction of being the smallest city in the nation. Vergennes and Middlebury to the south (population 7,500) function as trade centers for Addison County. Clean industries dominate the local economies: approximately 47 percent of Vergennes' work force is employed at Simmons Precision, manufacturer of aerospace fuel measurement systems, and Middlebury College, Kraft Foods and Polymers Plastics account for most of Middlebury's employment picture. The latter town is also the home of the Vermont State Craft Center, which provides a showcase for artisans from around the state.

Middlebury is perhaps best known for Middlebury College, a small, prestigious, liberal arts institution with an enrollment of 1,900 students. Founded in 1800 as an all-male school, Middlebury was one of the first colleges in the nation to become co-ed when it admitted women in the late 1800s. It is best known for its foreign language and English programs; both the summer Language School and the Bread Loaf Writer's Conference are internationally famous. The school campus arguably is one of the most beautiful in the state, perhaps even the nation, with its spacious lawns, walkways lined with arching trees and the plain but gracefully impressive buildings, all built of the same gray limestone, locally quarried.

Despite the dominance of the manufacturing and service industries in this region, the Lake Champlain Lowlands also are Vermont's prime agricultural country. Ask in Enosburg Falls what people there do for a living; the answer is simple and short: farming. The same would be true in dozens of other towns, from Panton and Shoreham to Grand Isle and Franklin. The fertile lowlands and relatively benign climate have given this region four of the five Class One agricultural counties in the state. Grand Isle ranks first, followed by Addison and Franklin counties. For example, 50 percent of Addison County is devoted to farming; this county alone accounts for 20 percent of the state's total marketable agricultural products. Even Chittenden County, with its large manufacturing segment, has more than one third of its area in active farm use, making it the fifth-ranking agricultural county in the state. The most purely agricultural town in the state is Panton, just west of Vergennes on the shore of Lake Champlain.

Dairying is the major farm occupation and most of its products go outside the state. Fluid milk is the pri-

mary export; even farms near the Canadian border send milk to markets in Boston and its surrounding suburbs. Milk production is so big here that the St. Albans Dairy Co-op is the ninth largest Vermont-based company in the state.

After fluid milk, cheese is an important product of the region's dairy operations, mostly to be exported. As one illustration, Baker's cheese manufactured at the Franklin County Cheese Plant in Enosburg Falls is sold primarily to bakeries in New York City. For many smaller communities, dairy farming (and milk products) are the backbone of the local economy. The largest employer in Hinesburg is the International Cheese Factory with 130 workers. The plant puts more than a million gallons of locally-produced milk into 150,000 pounds of cheese, every day.

Raising beef-cattle and sheep both have been increasing in importance over the last 10 years. Addison County leads the state in the number of cattle and calves with 64,653 in 1986; it also had 3,000 sheep. Still, this

is a far cry from the glory days of the merino sheep in the 1800s, when more than 1.6 million grazed Vermont's hillsides.

While dairying and stock-growing dominate regional farming, the Champlain fruit orchards also are a significant component of the agricultural picture. The groves of mostly apple trees are relatively common near the lake. Addison County leads the state with nearly two times more producing trees than any other county. Grand Isle and Chittenden counties also are important fruit growing areas, but on a much smaller scale than Addison. The proximity of a large body of water, which heats up slowly in the spring and is slow to cool in the autumn, moderates the local climate, preventing late frosts and early flowering.

Small sawmills can be found scattered throughout the region, and logging does figure into the local economies of quite a few towns, but nowhere does the timber industry dominate as it does in other parts of the country. Instead, the forests probably play a larger role

Above: The IBM complex at Essex Junction is the largest employer in the state and is one of many high-tech companies that have located in the Champlain lowlands.

Left: Such signs are familiar sights along back roads in the Champlain lowlands. Addison County alone accounts for 20 percent of the state's marketable agricultural products. GEORGE WUERTHNER PHOTOS

63

Top left: Slabs of limestone mark the edge of a large fault that delineates the Lake Champlain basin. Lake Champlain is the sixth largest freshwater lake in the country and often is referred to as the sixth Great Lake. GEORGE WUERTHNER

Top right: Vermont's economic boom has provided a market for the work of many craftsmen like this potter near Underhill. JOHN LYNCH

Right: Burlington's controversial McNeil Power Plant is the largest wood-burning electrical generation operation in the country. GEORGE WUERTHNER

Facing page: Boat dock at Malletts Bay on Lake Champlain. Lake Champlain has changed from primarily a working lake to a recreational one enjoyed year-round by residents. JOHN LYNCH

in tourism and recreation, attracting people to admire the fall colors, and delighting those who come to hike the mountains or ski the slopes.

Recreation Year-Round

Although ski development has occurred largely outside of this region, the Champlain Lowlands contain several smaller areas, including Middlebury College Snow Bowl and Bolton Valley Ski Area. Just beyond the region's boundaries are Jay Peak near Montgomery, where nearly 80 percent of the skiers are Canadian, the Stowe area and the Sugarbush area ski resorts— all three of which are less than an hour's drive from downtown Burlington. Undoubtedly the proximity of these big ski centers brings significant financial reward to the region.

Summer recreation, focused on and around the region's lakes— particularly Champlain— is important to both local residents and visitors. The popularity of the Champlain region as a place to relax and retire has brought many changes. Many summer "camps," for example, are being converted into year-round residences, placing a strain on local services and schools. One notable fact is that more than half the vacation homes are owned by Vermont residents; this is a higher percentage than anywhere else in the state. New Yorkers are the second largest group of second home owners, except in Grand Isle and Franklin counties where 25 percent of the homes are owned by Canadians.

The great Lake Champlain itself is undeniably one of the main attractions of the region. It is 110 miles long and 12 miles across at its widest point, but it narrows to less than a mile's width at its southern extremity. The 545 miles of shoreline make Champlain one of the largest freshwater lakes in the United States and it is often called the "sixth Great Lake." Like the true Great Lakes, Champlain is partly in Canada and empties north via the Richelieu River to the St. Lawrence, near Montreal.

The fisheries of the lake are outstanding. The successful story of the Lake Champlain fisheries restoration is due to a cooperative effort of the U.S. Fish and Wildlife Service and the states of Vermont and New York, which worked to bring back the once abundant lake trout and landlocked salmon. More than 3 million juvenile salmon and lake trout were stocked, and the fish have grown at an amazing rate. A two-year-old salmon may average five pounds. To expand this restoration program, the Vermont Fish and Game Department unveiled plans for a new fish hatchery at Kingsland Bay in 1982. The proposed hatchery has run into opposition, however, from some Lake Champlain residents who fear the operation will discharge pollutants into the lake.

The Kingsland Bay hatchery controversy is only part of a growing concern about development and its impacts on Lake Champlain. Water pollution, particularly the addition of phosphorous, spurs algal growth and the eutrophication of the lake. Eutrophication occurs when high algae densities reduce water transparency and deplete dissolved oxygen levels, which in turn can affect fish populations. Excessive algal growth, appearing on the surface as a green scum, also reduces the water's aesthetic appeal. Phosphorus pollution is the result of, among various causes, farmland run-off, sewage discharge and leaking septic systems.

With its still-generous supply of relatively flat space for the expansion of housing and industry, and with the region's proximity to both beautiful land- and water-scapes and superb recreational opportunities, the Lake Champlain Lowlands likely will continue to lead the state in economic level and in population total.

BURLINGTON

There are few U.S. cities with a more beautiful natural setting than Burlington. Located on a hill overlooking a wide, protected bay on Lake Champlain, with views across the water of New York's Adirondack Mountains, Burlington was recognized early as an attractive place to live. One of Burlington's first settlers was Ira Allen, who foresaw that "Burlington would...become a place of consequence." More than 200 years after Allen built a saw-mill and fort on the banks of the Winooski River, Burlington and its surrounding towns are the unqualified cultural, economic and educational heart of the state.

Its rise as a trading and transportation center made Burlington a likely British target during the War of 1812. Consequently, the U.S. Army fortified the port by placing cannons on the hill overlooking the bay. The site is now known as Battery Park. Buildings at the newly founded University of Vermont served as army barracks. The city was attacked by British boats in 1813, but incurred only minor damage.

Construction of the Champlain Canal linked the lake with the Hudson River and New York markets, and the port's traffic surged. Railroad transport later diminished the importance of lake transportation and Burlington might have slipped into a steady economic decline had it not been for the construction of a lumber planing mill in 1856. Other mills followed and Burlington was soon exporting vast quantities of lumber. By 1873 it was the third leading lumber port in the nation, with timber from Vermont as well as Canada.

Western competition and the Dingley Tariff Act of 1897, which decreased Canadian timber supplies, meant the decline of the city's mills. But these were replaced by textile mills, fine printing and the manufacture of electrical equipment, furniture and clothing. The city underwent new growth during World War II when its textile mills were called on to produce cloth for the war effort. In 1940 a branch of Bell Aircraft, subsequently taken over by General Electric, located in the town and began the trend towards light manufacturing. With the siting of an IBM plant in 1957 in adjacent Essex Junction, the city was confirmed as a high-tech, clean-industry business center.

Today the Queen City is the heart of Greater Burlington, rated as the 18th most livable city out of 329 metropolitan areas in the country. The ranking was based on factors such as climate, housing, health care, education, economy and recreation. The area would have rated much higher except for its dour climate, which is excessively cloudy (the skies are overcast above Burlington 53 percent of the time).

Like many cities, Burlington has felt the loss of industry to the suburbs and the lessening of the tax base. The city's ability to maintain public services is strained. Nevertheless, Burlington's urban core has sustained itself better than those of most larger cities. The down-town area has seen a revival with the construction of many high-rise office buildings and the restoration of many historic buildings, which now house more offices, shops and restaurants. The heart of this redevelopment is Church Street Marketplace, a four-block-long pedestrian mall with outdoor cafes and more than 100 stores.

One of Burlington's most precious assets undoubtedly is Lake Champlain. It provides year-round recreational opportunities—from boating, fishing, sailing and swimming in summer, to ice fishing and skating in the winter. It is the focal point of the city, providing sparkling blue vistas and marvelous sunsets silhouetting the Adirondacks. Its great value to Burlington is undeniable, but the question of what to do with the city's waterfront has become a major political controversy. Once the domain of

oil-tanks and warehouses, the waterfront is slowly experiencing a renaissance. While most residents welcome this in general, the specifics of the redevelopment plans are hotly debated. With the election of Socialist mayor Bernie Sanders, the impetus for a type of waterfront development benefitting all Burlington citizens was strengthened. But projects remain in limbo until there can be agreement on just what will be built, how to build it and, most importantly, who will pay for it.

Innovation is one of Burlington's key traits, as might be expected for the social and intellectual center of the state. One recent project, still under skeptical scrutiny, is a $66 million wood-burning power plant—the first municipal operation of its kind in the nation. But the new plant has had problems. New power sources, primarily Quebec hydro-electric, have undercut the profitability of wood power-generation.

Burlington is the state's major educational center. More than 13,500 students are enrolled in local institutions, including Champlain College, Burlington College, Trinity College, and St. Michael's College in nearby Winooski.

In addition to these private schools, Burlington is home to the University of Vermont, founded in 1791 when Ira Allen donated 50 acres on which to build the new college. Today more than 9,200 students attend UVM, which is unique among state universities in that student tuition payments cover a large proportion of the total operating costs. In addition, a high percentage of students are out-of-state residents, who are attracted by the school's reputation for Ivy League-level educational quality, as well as its easy access to recreational amenities.

The presence of so many institutions of higher education and well-paid professionals working in the city ensures strong support for cultural activities, including theater, music and lectures. Burlington hosts, among other events and organizations, the Champlain Shakespeare Festival, the Discover Jazz Festival, the Vermont Symphony Orchestra and the UVM Baroque Ensemble.

Greater Burlington also supports a diversity of economic opportunities. Among the larger employers are the city, state and federal governments, UVM, IBM, General Electric, Digital Equipment, New England Telephone, Rossignol Ski Company and Lane Press. The region's bustling economy has helped the construction industry; Pizzagalli Construction Company alone has 1,300 workers.

Despite the dilemmas of rapid growth, Burlington remains a popular place to locate, a stimulating center of cultural diversity and intellectual inventiveness. Its position as the state's economic leader is not likely to be challenged in the near future. It promises to stay true to its appellation as the "Queen City."

Top: Lake Champlain is certainly Burlington's greatest natural resource, providing recreation in winter and summer as well as lovely vistas.
Above: University of Vermont campus.
Left: Church Street Marketplace in downtown Burlington.
GEORGE WUERTHNER PHOTOS

CHAPTER SEVEN

SOUTHWEST REGION

Diversity is the hallmark of Vermont's Southwest region. Taking in Rutland and Bennington counties, it is physically characterized by the north-south Valley of Vermont— a major travel corridor running the length of the region— bounded by significant uplands on either side. The Taconic Range on the Vermont/New York border offers routes of passage where westward-flowing rivers cut through the rugged hills. The Green Mountains, rising steeply on the east side of the valley, form a high, continuous plateau here, with several emergent peaks along the crest; the range remains to this day a notable hindrance to travel to and from the other side of the state.

The Valley of Vermont is fairly narrow along much of its length, reaching its most constricted point about midway, near Danby and at the hydrographic divide between Otter Creek— the longest river contained entirely in the state— and Batten Kill, a trout stream of considerable fame. The region's two major communities, Rutland and Bennington (from which the county names are derived), sit in especially broad sections of the valley, afforded a sense of space that— except for in the Champlain Lowlands— is unusual for the state. Given the advantages of this relative openness as well as their strategic locations, Rutland (approximate population 26,000) and Bennington (nearly 16,000 residents) long have ranked second and third respectively among the state's largest municipalities. Both physically and economically, they dominate the northern and southern ends of the region and have begun to sprawl outwards beyond city limits, though admittedly on a smaller scale than booming Burlington.

The balance of the region's population resides mostly in the small communities surrounding the main centers, or in more remote locations in the hinterlands. Of note are a few secondary centers: Manchester, a burgeoning "yuppie" resort nurtured by both winter and summer vacationers; Brandon, a local trade center on the north Rutland county border; and the neighboring towns of Fair Haven and Poultney, once focused on slate quarrying and now serving an important summer home and recreation area, where there is a local concentration of fine lakes.

White trunks of paper birch dominate a forest in the Taconic Mountains. GEORGE WUERTHNER

Facing page, left: Red trillium—a common spring wildflower. MOLLIE MATTESON

Right: Three physiographic landforms—the Valley of Vermont, the Taconic and the Green mountains— characterize southwest Vermont. All are represented in this photo taken from Baker Peak in the Green Mountains, looking west to the Taconics across the Valley of Vermont. GEORGE WUERTHNER

The Southwest's landscapes run the gamut from mountain wilderness in the Green Mountain National Forest to rural countryside and old-fashioned villages, to a pair of bustling commercial centers. Besides Bennington and Rutland and the secondary centers strung along the main arteries in the valley and along the Castleton River, there are small, poor mountain hamlets, like Woodford and Readsboro. There are small, wealthy upland hamlets as well: Landgrove, east of the Green Mountain crest, is an example. Tidy, restored hill farms dot country roads as on a color postcard. Most of the Southwest region is noticeably lacking in wide expanses of water, though streams are in abundance. The pocket of lake country around Fair Haven, Poultney and Castleton is an exception. Lake Bomoseen is the largest body of water completely within Vermont's borders. Lake Hortonia and Lake St. Catherine, too, have their charms, as the dense ring of summer cabins around them testifies.

This physical diversity is verified by the varied economy— strongest in manufacturing, but increasingly dependent on service and trade and the recreation industry. Farming and quarrying remain in evidence along the western edge of the region but neither figures significantly in the overall economic picture. Locally, agricultural activity is notable in the Mettawee and Poultney river valleys. Marble is still being extracted from Dorset Mountain in Danby and a quarry in West Rutland; a few slate companies operate out of Pawlet, Fair Haven and Poultney along with several based in Granville, New York just over the state line; calcium carbonate— used in white pigment and as a filler material— is quarried in South Wallingford and processed in Florence, north of Rutland.

A Dramatic Past

The mosaic of scenery and human activity characterizing the region today is lent an added dimension by its dramatic past, in which a number of key events were crucial not only to Vermont's destiny, but also to that of the young nation of America. While many prominent places and routes of yesteryear have fallen into obscurity, a few have remained significant throughout the state's history, or have risen again to the limelight. For example, in 1730 fur trader James Cross described the traditional Indian route along Otter Creek and the fertile country around it, abundantly stocked with beaver. Later, the flat valley of Otter Creek became a way for soldiers during the French and Indian wars. British and American troops built the Crown Point Military Road in that same period, from Lake Champlain across the mountains to the Connecticut River Valley. Today both Otter Creek and the military road are closely paralleled by modern highways for much of their lengths. Where the two early footpaths intersected, in the broad lowlands where trader James Cross found so many beaver, today flourishes the city of Rutland. It is also a major junction on the cross-state Route 4 that passes through the Killington-Pico ski area.

The Southwest region figured prominently during Revolutionary times, being the stomping grounds of Vermont's rowdy, rebellious Green Mountain Boys, and directly adjacent to the much-hated, threatening commonwealth of New York. The Green Mountain Boys, known by their detractors as the "Bennington Mob," officially formed in that town in 1770 at Fay's Catamount Tavern. Though the building is gone, the stuffed panther that stood outside, its face symbolically frozen in a defiant snarl directed towards the western border, is remembered with a modern bronze version.

In 1775, the Boys met at Castleton to plan the capture of Fort Ticonderoga. Another tavern served as headquarters for the operation. In haste to round up recruits, Ethan Allen sent a Chittenden town grantee, one Gershom Beach, to the surrounding communities. He did Paul Revere one better: he didn't ride, he ran.

At a Dorset tavern in 1776, the Green Mountain Boys first issued a Vermont declaration of independence.

Southwest Vermont was the locus of several critical events in 1777. American troops at Fort Ticonderoga retreated in the face of strengthening British forces to the north. On July 7, enemy forces including Hessian mercenaries and British-allied Indians met the Americans at Hubbardton. Seth Warner led the Green Mountain Boys alongside regiments from Massachusetts and New Hampshire. The town of Hubbardton was burned and the Americans were routed. It was the only Revolutionary War battle actually fought in Vermont.

Governor Thomas Chittenden also left his northern home for a confiscated Tory estate in Arlington. During

the Revolutionary period, he made this the de facto seat of Vermont's government. It was in the adjacent town of Manchester that Ira Allen formally proposed that Tory homes be seized and used to raise money for the war effort. Arlington's "Tory Hollow" had many such sequestered properties.

August 16, 1777 marked a major turning point in Burgoyne's invasion. A contingent under Colonel Baum, commissioned to capture supplies at a storehouse in Bennington, clashed with Americans a few miles west of town. The militiamen led by General John Stark, including the Green Mountain Boys, defeated the enemy troops on a hill overlooking the Walloomsac River, in Hoosick, New York. Today, the yearly anniversary of the Battle of Bennington is a state holiday, celebrated with parades, fireworks and battle re-enactments— Vermont's second Fourth of July.

Following the revolution, the northern reaches of Vermont were repopulated, and new settlers arrived. In the Southwest region distinctive industries already were developing. In Dorset, the first marble quarry in North America was initiated in 1785. The Bennington Pottery company began in 1793, producing the unique and un-

mistakable ceramics that today are treasured collector's items. Kaolin deposits on the east side of the town were the raw material source for the clay wares. Slate was also being quarried near Fair Haven, Castleton and Poultney as early as the late 1700s.

As in many other parts of the state, the Southwest saw the hills cleared and peppered with flocks of Merino sheep, beginning in the early 19th century. By 1840, Bennington County had a sheep density of 159 per square mile; Rutland County had 292. Although not so suitable for grazing as the Champlain lowlands, the southwest sheep farms were helped by their proximity to a growing textile industry in Bennington.

Cloth and Stone

Textiles were the first true manufacturing industry in Vermont; though, compared to the giant factories in more industrialized southern New England, Green Mountain mills were small. Factories were scattered throughout the state, but among them Bennington was the major center in terms of number of firms and total employed. In most of the rest of the state, wool process-

Left: Snowshoer ascends a slope in the Green Mountains overlooking the Valley of Vermont near its narrowest point opposite the Taconics' Dorset Mountain.

Above: Vermont's strict sign laws have led to the development of many colorful and beautiful signs such as this, which graces the Shaftsbury Country Store. GEORGE WUERTHNER PHOTOS

Facing page, top: The Mettawee River Valley is one of Southwest Vermont's most important agricultural regions.

Bottom: Marble as white as the snow that covers it lies piled at the Vermont Marble Company plant in Proctor. GEORGE WUERTHNER PHOTOS

71

NORMAN ROCKWELL

Norman Rockwell contributed perhaps more than anyone else to the popular vision of Vermont. Although not a native, he lived and worked in the small town of Arlington from 1939 to 1953, before moving to Stockbridge, Massachusetts. His tenure in Arlington often is considered to have been during the pinnacle of his career, when he painted his most famous work, known as the "Four Freedoms."

Rockwell's universal appeal stems from his uncanny ability to capture real people doing everyday things. His paintings strike chords of recognition in all of us. In the faces he portrays, we may see someone we love and know—perhaps even ourselves—the shy adolescent gathering the nerve to kiss his girlfriend, the relaxed family with members of all ages, seated 'round the Thanksgiving turkey—evoke a feeling of familiarity and remind us of the humanity we all share.

Rockwell was born in 1894 in New York City, where he spent his youth and young adulthood. Each summer when he was a boy, however, his family vacationed on rural New England farms and gave Rockwell his first taste of small-town life, which would figure so prominently in the subject matter of his painting career. He dropped out of high school to devote himself to painting, and by age 19 was named art director for Boy's Life magazine. At 22 years of age he was painting covers for the Saturday Evening Post, He eventually created 321 Post covers.

He was 45 years old and on his second marriage when he finally moved from New York to Vermont to live out his childhood fantasy of dwelling in the country. Rockwell bought a farm on the Batten Kill River just west of Arlington, and soon became a well known and liked local personality. The authenticity of Rockwell's paintings is due in part to his use of neighbors and fellow townspeople as models. Rockwell recruited the local residents he wished to paint, then posed them to suit the current work. A photographer took pictures of the models, so that their expressions and mannerisms could be captured exactly. Although Rockwell relied on his imagination to provide inspiration and themes, he studied the photographs painstakingly in order to recreate the authentic look. The grease on the mechanic's hand, the creases in an old-timer's hat, were the special touches that made Rockwell's art ring true.

This attention to detail is demonstrated by a Post cover showing a schoolgirl with a black eye waiting outside the principal's office. From her self-satisfied grin, it is obvious she won the fight. To make the painting, Rockwell advertised that he would pay five dollars to a model with a real black eye. Eventually he found a boy with an appropriate shiner and transferred the image to the female character he envisioned.

"Christmas Homecoming" was a Saturday Evening Post cover in 1945. Posing beside the original is Mary Immen Hall, the model for the blond teenager at the extreme right of the painting. She was a classmate of Thomas Rockwell and spent much time with the family, all of whom are portrayed here. Norman Rockwell, with his pipe, looks on as his wife Mary welcomes their oldest son, Jarvis. Thomas, in plaid shirt, is behind his mother; beside him in black is a family friend, the painter Grandma Moses, and Peter Rockwell is at the extreme left. According to Ms. Hall, the twins are modeled on a neighbor, Sharon O'Neil, whom Rockwell said he liked so much he portrayed her as two little girls. PHOTO COURTESY OF THE ARLINGTON GALLERY, ARLINGTON, VT. SATURDAY EVENING POST COVER OF 12/28/45 COPYRIGHT © 1945 ESTATE OF NORMAN ROCKWELL.

Art critics never approved of Rockwell's work, but his popularity still holds strong, even after his death, in 1978 at age 84. His paintings stay fresh and delightful because his characters are involved in timeless human emotions and events. Families still gather for the holidays, baseball still is played in the city park, and teenagers still are awkward in first love. Although Rockwell lived in Vermont only for 14 years, he captured the traits of hopefulness, vitality and fortitude that are part of the famed Vermont character. Rockwell's art always will be a Green Mountain State treasure.

ing was the major enterprise, but Bennington's primary product was cotton cloth and, by the mid-18th century, knitwear of both wool and cotton. Competition from factories in America's South hurt New England businesses even before the Civil War, but more-remote Vermont, with its tradition of low wages, held onto its textile industry into the 1930s and '40s. From 1910 until after 1920, Bennington had approximately 2,300 workers in textiles. But by 1938, the largest single employer in town was gone. The "Big Mill" close-down put one fourth of the town's employed out on the streets. By 1950, only 200 people were employed in the industry. Today, most of the old plants are occupied by other manufacturers; new companies in new industrial parks also have contributed to the maintenance of Bennington's vital manufacturing economy. Their products include machine tools and parts, batteries and electronic components.

The slate and marble quarries in and around the Rutland area were responsible for the town's steady but slow growth, from the early 1800s to mid-century. It was not until the arrival of the railroad in 1849, however, that these industries boomed and led to the tripling of Rutland's population between 1850 and 1880. By the latter date, Rutland surpassed Burlington with 12,149 residents, making it the largest community in Vermont for the first and only time in its history.

Vermont marble production was transformed from a small time, father-and-son operation to a major industry of world significance largely at the hands of one man—Colonel Redfield Proctor. Returning a hero from the Civil War, he bought up the small shops and companies and expanded his enterprise—the Vermont Marble Company—until he controlled a large portion of the national marble business. By 1886, the Proctor empire wielded such influence over the village of then-Sutherland Falls that it was made a town in its own right, cut out of the township of Rutland and stamped with the name of the man who had taken it from backwater obscurity to global fame. Proctor himself served as governor of Vermont, U.S. senator, and Secretary of War under President Benjamin Harrison. Two of his sons also became governors, as did several chief executives of the company. The Proctor dynasty held sway in the state for nearly a century.

The economic boom meant a demand for more laborers—on the railroads, in the quarries, in manufacturing. Irish immigrants helped to put in many miles of Vermont track. Skilled stonecutters from Italy, Poland, Sweden and Scotland came to work the marble; in 1910,

2.6 percent of Rutland County residents were native Italians. The slate towns attracted Welsh stoneworkers. In 1877, the Howe Scale Works moved from Brandon to Rutland and secured the future of manufacturing in that city. Along with the railroads and the marble industry, Howe Scale was a major employer in Rutland for many years. By the end of World War II, the Howe company employed some 800 workers.

In the state as a whole, tourism ranks second in the economic hierarchy. For the Southwest corner particularly, the pursuit of recreation and leisure long has had a considerable influence on the economy, the social make-up and layout of communities, even the look of the land itself. As the interstate highways have speeded travel to more northerly points, the popularity of such places as Stowe and the Mad River Valley has risen as well.

From a graveyard in Shaftsbury, looking toward Mt. Glastenbury in the Green Mountains. The relative age of graveyards can be gauged by the kind of stone used for memorials. Prior to 1900, when granite became popular, limestone and marble were the preferred materials. GEORGE WUERTHNER

Above: The Clarendon Springs Hotel
as it appeared during its heyday in
the late 1800s .
VERMONT HISTORICAL SOCIETY
Right: Fishing the Batten Kill,
Vermont's most famous trout stream.
GEORGE WUERTHNER
Top: Orvis Fly Rod company in
Manchester. GEORGE WUERTHNER

Facing page, top: Loading logs near
Shaftsbury. Most of Vermont's timberlands are held privately by many
small-woodlot owners.

Right: The elegant Equinox Hotel,
which boasts marble sidewalks, is
the centerpiece for Manchester,
one of Vermont's poshest resort
towns. GEORGE WUERTHNER PHOTOS

Spas and Skis

The search for health and quick cures is hardly
new. Only the remedies change, along with scientific
progress and whims of fashion. In 1776, a self-pro-
claimed clairvoyant named Asa Smith declared the waters of a mineral spring at Clarendon to have strong
healing powers. In its heyday, which lasted some 50
years, Clarendon Springs was purported to have cured
sufferers of "salt rheum, scrofula, cancer [and] infertili-
ty." There, as at Middletown Springs, Equinox Springs in
Manchester and elsewhere in the state, a spacious hotel
housed the patient-vacationers. When the medicinal
waters fell into disfavor among the health-seekers, so did
the resorts that depended on them. The hotel at Clarendon has been somewhat restored, but the structure at
Middletown has been replaced by trees. The grand
Equinox Inn, which once hosted— among other famous
guests— Mrs. Abraham Lincoln and Mrs. Ulysses Grant,
closed in 1973 after a long period of decay. The recent
revitalization of Manchester, which never completely
faded as a resort town, has seen the accompanying $20
million restoration of the palatial building, which re-
opened in 1985.

The first "tourists" to Vermont, then, were the
health spa visitors. Yet Vermont was never so famous
nor prestigious a vacation spot as Saratoga Springs in
New York, or the plush Atlantic seaside resorts. Neither
did the Green Mountains have the expanse and wildness
of the White Mountains or the Adirondacks. After the
Civil War, the mineral-spring resorts gradually declined.
Perhaps it was the loss of Southern clients, upon whom
Clarendon in particular had depended. Or perhaps, more
simply, the mineral springs went out of fashion. But new
fashions always move in to take the place of the old, and
today Southwest Vermont is a very "in" place to be.

In 1937, Bromley Mountain became the first ski
area development in Southwest Vermont. Skiers rode up
the mountain, east of Manchester near the town of Peru,

by clinging to one of several rope tows. In 1940, the first chairlift was constructed at Stowe on Mt. Mansfield and the industry was on its way. Pico also opened in 1937, and partnered with big-brother Killington, which started business in 1957, the joint resort area probably draws the most visitors in the state. Killington boasts the greatest vertical drop in the state (3,000') and the longest season in the Northeast. It claims to have the longest gondola line in the country and the most extensive snowmaking operation in the world. The changes that have accompanied the explosion of the ski industry are enormous in both degree and number. When Killington first sent schussers down the slopes above the little logging hamlet of Sherburne Center, it barely was a wide spot in the road. Today, the narrow valley— hardly more than a deep ravine in some places— echoes with the throb of motors and the restless come-and-go of skiers and lookers. Unlike Manchester, a four-season resort town with a solid central core and still surrounded by many acres of developable valley bottom, Killington is strung out along the highway and the area is rapidly running out of flat ground on which to build. In 1973— the last time a count was made— there were some 781 vacation homes in and around Killington-Pico. Since then, many more have been built, and a growing proportion of them are year-round residences.

It was uncontrolled, mushrooming growth of another Vermont ski region that finally spurred the passage of the landmark Act 250 law almost two decades ago. At issue for the Killington area is the sanctity of a 3,000-acre undeveloped parcel called Parker's Gore, a critical area for black bears, the water quality of streams that originate around Killington and protection of the Long/Appalachian Trail corridor, which passes through a potential link-up zone between Killington's and Pico's ski trail systems. Killington's plans are extensive, and include eight to 10 new chairlifts, more trails and snow-making reservoirs, pump stations, lodges and 2,000 to 3,000 condominiums that will require sewage treatment facilities and extension of the current water, electricity and highway lines. Parker's Gore, an odd-shaped section of land left out of early surveyors' maps, sits on the crest of the Green Mountains, and is said to contain prime habitat for black bears as well as bobcats, fishers and minks. The Vermont Department of Fish and Wildlife is in the process of formally identifying and protecting the bears' habitat, which could include large tracts of high-elevation land and important travel corridors. In the Killington ski area, Parker's Gore is part of a 18,500-acre habitat being studied by the state. It is owned by Killington Ltd. and International Paper Realty Company and is the site of a recently proposed snow-making pond. Proponents of development claim that the black bear is merely a convenient weapon with which conservationists are blocking ski-area expansion. Environmentalists counter that the pond is merely the first step in a major plan to drastically change the area.

Also of concern is the volume of water that may potentially be withdrawn from the Ottauquechee River drainage. Minimum flow levels are required to dilute downstream effluents to Class B water-quality standards. The Ottauquechee is a tributary of the Connecticut River, the lower reaches of which are now experiencing the return of the Atlantic salmon. Someday the Ottauquechee again may host the sea-going fish, but only if it maintains an acceptably clean watery habitat.

With Southwest Vermont primed to receive new, strategic miles of superhighway— the western connector to Bennington from New York state, the extension of new Route 7 between Manchester and Dorset, going eventually to Wallingford— the future can promise only continued growth and accessibility for more-populated neighbor states. Whether this region, with the exploding Burlington complex to the north, will be able— or want— to avoid the urban/suburban "sprawlitis" that is infecting many parts of the nation, will depend partly on the will of Vermonters. But as has been demonstrated repeatedly in its past, the southwest corner is not full sovereign over its destiny. Whatever direction the rest of the Northeast goes in the years ahead, the people of Southwest Vermont will be among the first to feel the tugging strings.

Skiing at Bromley Mountain.
GEORGE WUERTHNER

BENNINGTON

Where the Valley of Vermont broadens into an open, rolling basin, bounded by wooded mountains and hilly slopes planted in apple orchards, there— in the state's southwest corner— sits historical Bennington. When the colonial governor of New Hampshire, Benning Wentworth, chose this site for his first grant in the disputed territory that later would be called Vermont, he did not choose arbitrarily. Less than 20 miles from the Hudson River, and at one terminus of the long, low Valley of Vermont— a natural travel corridor— the town always has held a strategic position in the march of events, people and commerce through the Green Mountain state.

Because of Bennington's proximity to southern New England, it was the port of entry for settlers and the goods they needed. Its location made it an important trade center, and here manufacturing was viable early on because out-of-state markets were close. Paper, iron and pottery were being produced before the 19th century. In the mid-1800s, the arrival of the railroads

made Bennington, already producing woolen yarns and fabrics, a textile center. In this century, machine parts, batteries, industrial fabrics and skiwear are among the host of Bennington's various products.

Today about one in three working Benningtonians is in manufacturing. Parts of the service industry, including tourism, and retail and wholesale trade, each employs about one quarter of the area's labor force. With

expensive four-year institution in the country. Its annual tuition is now more than $18,000. Drawing many of its students from the New York metropolitan area, it long has been something of an island of liberal intellectualism in a sea of proletarian pragmatism. While the college remains—in the minds of most Benningtonians—the place "up there," community leaders and college administrators continue to work at bringing town and gown closer.

Ironically, perhaps the greatest threat to Bennington—as a distinctive community—is the very thing that was responsible for its early prominence and later prosperity. Its proximity to more densely populated areas, especially the Albany, New York "Capital District"

with nearly a million residents, makes Bennington an attractive site for those who may wish to "live in the country" but be not too far from city goods, services and jobs. As the margins of the Albany urban area push outwards, there are fears that Bennington soon will be where Benningtonians sleep, but not where they work. The so-called "Western Connector" highway, now an inevitability, will make the 40 miles to the Capital District even shorter than they are now.

the remainder of the town's employed scattered in other sectors, Bennington rests on a fairly diverse, healthy economic foundation.

The original village of Bennington, now called Old Bennington, is aligned mostly along one street, which rises to the grounds of the Bennington Battle Monument and the 300' obelisk itself. The row of fresh white colonial homes and the graceful Old First Church (the oldest church in the state) form a New England picture-postcard classic, while the towering stone spire at the top of the hill is Bennington's unique landmark, visible almost anywhere in the valley.

Bennington College occupies a grassy knoll in North Bennington. An innovative, non-traditional school, with special emphasis on the arts and dance, it has gained national notice as the most

CHAPTER EIGHT

ESSENTIAL SOUTHEAST

Within this narrow band of rolling hills, bounded by the Connecticut River and the Green Mountain range, is the distillation of New England: as it once was and as we may wish it still were. Embodied in the land- and people-scapes of Southeast Vermont is the essence of an ideal, and a remembrance, of our nation's beginnings and development. Despite the relatively recent incursions of fast-track, computer-age America, the sense of yesteryear still is strong and uncorrupted here in Windham and Windsor counties, and this area offers perhaps the clearest and most unobstructed view in all of New England of its distinctive past.

Similarly, the Connecticut River does not impress the first-time viewer with its breadth or grandeur. Among the mighty rivers that led Americans to new frontiers— the Hudson, the Delaware, the Ohio and so on— this is a rather thin and humble stream. The upper Connecticut valley is broader than those of the tributaries draining the Vermont piedmont; nonetheless the river bottom-land is limited, and the hills on either side rise fairly quickly, though they are not high. The river itself, subdued by dams, flows obediently and without flourish.

In keeping with the modest nature of the landscape in this part of the state, the east slope of the Green Mountains is so gradual as to be nearly indistinguishable from the docile troughs and swells of the piedmont. No clear demarcation line separates one zone from the other, although a few summits in the southern range stick up above the general high surface of the range. Most of these— Stratton, Mt. Snow, Haystack Mountain— wear the fanlike stripings of ski areas.

The human elements of this gentle landscape, from farms to factories, also are representative of the many facets of the New England history and character that have mostly faded from view elsewhere. Puritan-white clapboard houses encircle a grassy village green; long, warped and weathered covered bridges of graying wood defy gravity and the Vermont highway department; connected house and barn structures, designed to preserve the Yankee farmer in the harsh New England winters, ramble next to the road or atop a cleared hill.

Industry Surrounded by Cows

But the pastoral, colonial flavor of the many hamlets and small towns in Southeast Vermont alone do not make this New England's "living museum." For when the poorer soils were depleted and no good ground was left to till, New England in the 19th century became industrial. And here, in Windsor, Springfield, Bellows Falls and Brattleboro, one can read this chapter of history, too, in the old brick plants, the power-producing waterfalls, the opulent mansions on the high streets and the factory rowhouses below.

U.S. Senator Ralph Flanders of Springfield once described his town as "an island of heavy industry completely surrounded by cows." Today there are fewer farms and many of the companies of the last century have closed down or relocated. But although the forces of an international economy have remade the southeast region's manufacturing towns, they have by no means diminished their importance as manufacturing centers. As a quick drive along Vermont's Connecticut River corridor will demonstrate, business is better than ever in the cradle of Vermont industry.

The opening of Southeast Vermont to settlement began early, in 1713, when Massachusetts gave the so-

Fall color along the Connecticut River, which separates Vermont and New Hampshire. JAMES RANDKLEV

Facing page, left: Strawberries.
TED LEVIN

Right: Farm near Reading in the rolling Vermont piedmont country.
JEFF GNASS

79

MONTEBELLO HOUSE,
SULPHUR AND IRON SPRINGS
AND
BATHING ESTABLISHMENT.
Newbury, Vermont.

Top: The longest covered bridge in Vermont spans the Connecticut River at Windsor. GEORGE WUERTHNER
Bottom: Early promotion for Montebello House. VERMONT HISTORICAL SOCIETY

called "Equivalent Lands" to Connecticut. The parcel included the area now within the towns of Putney, Dummerston, Vernon and Brattleboro, and was compensation for other lands, rightfully Connecticut's, that Massachusetts had mistakenly claimed and sold. Connecticut, in turn, sold the Equivalent Lands, a part of which eventually was acquired for speculative purposes by William Dummer, Lieutenant-Governor of Massachusetts, and a William Brattle.

The first permanent English settlement in the state was Fort Dummer, built in 1724 in the southeast corner of the present-day town of Brattleboro. It was commissioned by the colonial government of Massachusetts to protect towns to the south from parties of raiding Indians. Later, other forts were constructed on either side of the river, including two in Vernon.

The Green Mountain range, today a seemingly mild-mannered topographic wrinkle, demarcated a major division in the society and politics of early Vermont. East-side settlers came up the Connecticut River Valley; west-side Vermonters entered via the Valley of Vermont. East-siders typically arrived as entire families from eastern and central Massachusetts and Connecticut. Many were led by former soldiers who had worked on the Crown Point Military Road between the Connecticut River and Lake Champlain, and liked what they'd seen. By contrast, the opening of the west side of the Green Mountains was conducted by former residents of western New England and Rhode Island, among which were a considerable number of land speculators and profit

seekers. The east side was conservative, church-oriented and often loyal to the British crown. West-side society, which counted the Allen brothers, Seth Warner, Remember Baker and other members of the "Bennington Mob" among its distinguished citizenry, was less content to acquiesce to outside authority. Some might say that included divine authority as well: only two of the first 21 Congregational churches in Vermont were located on the west side. The other 19 were built by reverent inhabitants of the Connecticut Valley.

East-side settlements, buffered by the Green Mountains and the west-side strip, enjoyed relative stability and peace during the French and Indian War and the Revolutionary War. While their western neighbors battled New York officials and were forced to flee their homes in the face of enemy troops invading via the Lake Champlain Valley, eastern Vermonters were building and developing vigorous communities. Halifax, Dummerston, Putney and Westminster in southern Windham county all reached their maximum populations before 1810. In 1790 and 1800, Guilford, sandwiched between Vernon and Brattleboro, was the largest Vermont town with 2,400 inhabitants.

New York's "Cumberland"

The Southeast region, later to be divided into Windham County and its sister to the north, Windsor, was designated "Cumberland" in 1768 by the colony of New York. The rest of Vermont was subsequently divided into Gloucester and Albany counties. New York claimed jurisdiction over the entire territory and demanded that Vermonters exchange their original charters for grants from New York, for a small fee. Large land holders such as the Allen brothers were understandably resistant, but many Cumberland County residents obeyed willingly. In fact, one faction— centered around present-day Windham County— openly was loyal to New York.

Probably the majority of New Hampshire grant settlers in that unstable period before statehood were either ambivalent or opposed to the actions of the rebellious Green Mountain Boys. Many east-side residents feared and resented west-side dominance and supported the cause of Reverend Eleazar Wheelock, founder of Dartmouth College. Wheelock was the main proponent of Vermont annexation of a number of New Hampshire towns along the Connecticut River. This act would have offset the perceived political imbalance in the Green Mountain leadership corps. Interestingly, the 16 New Hampshire communities wishing to join the emerging republic believed they had no voice in their own government, which was centered in New Hampshire's south-eastern corner.

Not all Cumberland County settlers were pleased with New York governmental administration. In 1775, 100 angry farmers, threatened by foreclosure proceedings, attempted to block the meeting of the New York-appointed Cumberland County Court in Westminster. Armed with wooden clubs, they were confronted by a New York sheriff and his deputies, who in the mayhem shot two of the mobbers. The dead men became martyrs for both east- and west-side Vermonters, and the "Westminster Massacre"—which Ethan Allen and his cohorts shrewdly capitalized on—unified the territory in its hostility toward the "Yorkers."

Two years later at Westminster, leaders of the New Hampshire grants declared that theirs was an independent state. At that time they called it New Connecticut. Within half a year, the constitution was adopted at Windsor town, and the new, independent republic was called Vermont.

Ironically, although Windsor deems itself the "birthplace of Vermont," many towns in the southeast region did not support the constitution: again, their fear was of west-side domination. Brattleboro's veto of 165 votes to one against establishment of the new republic, illustrates how deeply sentiment ran in some communities. To appease these reluctant Green Mountain-ers, the Vermont legislature agreed to annex the 16 New Hampshire towns in 1778. One year later, however, the towns were dumped when it became obvious they were political liabilities to Vermont's campaign for statehood.

By the close of the 18th century, Vermont was firmly ensconced as a full member of the Union. Within one to two decades, most of the more accessible reaches of the state would see the peak of their growth and development—at least for the next century or more. The Connecticut River was not only a migration route for pioneers, but also a vital and important link to southern, industrializing New England. In 1802, the first canal in the country was finished at Bellows Falls, allowing flatboats to bypass the rapids there. By 1810, canals at White River Junction enabled boats to reach Wells River in Orange County.

Weathersfield Bow, a bend on the Connecticut north of Springfield, was the first place in the state to host merino sheep, imported from Portugal by American consul and amateur sheep breeder William Jarvis. At best, the subsequent sheep boom was a temporary boon to an already stagnating frontier economy. Many steep uplands were cleared to accommodate the voracious

Above photos: Signs add to the quaint appearances of many Vermont towns.

Left: Mark Rosenthal painstakingly constructs bamboo fly rods at his Springfield home.
GEORGE WUERTHNER PHOTOS

Above: A home in Chester, built of locally-quarried stone. ROBERT PERRON

Right: Waterfalls on the Black River provided power for the early industry of Springfield, which soon earned the nickname Precision Valley because of the many manufacturing and machine shops located there. GEORGE WUERTHNER

grazers, leading to severe soil erosion and stream degradation. Some of the worst overgrazing occurred in the southeast region and stirred Woodstock native George Perkins Marsh to compose his book on the destructive impacts of man on nature.

In the days when an abundance of flowing water meant a wealth of energy for industry, southeast Vermont was quite propitiously endowed. Mills sprouted along the Connecticut and its tributaries— the West River, the Williams, Saxtons, Black, Ottauquechee and White. They spun and wove into cloth the fleecy crop growing on the region's hillsides. Springfield and Bethel had sizable enterprises. Imported cotton also was made into cloth in Hartford, Weathersfield and Wilmington.

Precision Valley

The basic raw material of the region's most important and best-known industry was not wool, however, or anything else that could be farmed or logged or mined. It was ingenuity and a knack for tinkering that spawned

and nurtured Vermont's internationally-recognized machine tool production. The origins of the industry date back to 1827 when John Cooper of Guildhall invented a rotative water pump. His innovations went further than this, however, as he proposed to mass-produce certain components of his machine so that worn-out parts could be replaced with new, identical pieces. Previously, craftsmen had labored over each new item one at a time, making for slow, tedious work and unique, unstandardized creations. Cooper was one of the first to initiate the American system of interchangeable parts.

In 1828, he took out a patent on his machine to make machines that made his water pumps. A machinist, Asahel Hubbard of West Windsor, who took an interest and the two began the National Hydraulic Company in Windsor (with the backing of Jabez Proctor, father of another famous Vermont industrialist).

Inventiveness is contagious, apparently, for in 1835 Hubbard's son-in-law came up with a better rifle underhammer. Eventually National Hydraulic became Robbins and Lawrence, an arms maker supplying guns for westward-bound gold-seekers. Business truly boomed in 1851 when the company received a contract from the British to produce $25,000 worth of muskets as well as parts and machine tools with which to make the guns. The demand for the arms dropped suddenly at the end of Britain's Crimean War in 1856. Out of the demise of this firm was born another, Jones and Lamson, which would become perhaps the most famous machine-tool maker in the history of the industry.

But in the meantime the arms manufacturers enjoyed business brought by another war, this time America's own civil war. E.G. Lamson's shop in Windsor assembled the "Sharpe-shooter," named for its inventor as well for the firearm's deadly accuracy.

In 1888, Jones and Lamson was moved to Springfield, south of Windsor. It was a rather remote spot, located up the narrow Black River valley, six miles from the nearest railroad junction. But it was not long before the town was transformed by this firm, and its imaginative leadership, into the world center of the machine tool, or "precision," industry. James Hartness, a young inventor from Connecticut, was called to supervise Jones and Lamson's new shop. There, he put the finishing touches on his flat turret lathe, which became the company's chief product for a dozen years and brought Springfield wide recognition as "Precision Valley."

New ideas also constantly were being produced at the Jones and Lamson Company. With encouragement from the parent plant, several J and L tool designers went on to found their own firms in Springfield, spawning an entire family of machine-tool manufacturers. Fellows Gear Shaper started up in 1896; the Bryant Chucking Grinder Company was founded in 1909; the Lovejoy Tool Company followed in 1917. And in Windsor, invention remained a mainstay as well. Frank Cone, working at the Windsor Machine Company, designed a new type of lathe that he put into production the same year Lovejoy opened its doors.

But today business is truly international, and many American companies must compete not only with other domestic manufacturers, but also with foreign businesses. With formidable rivals like the Japanese, Jones and Lamson could no longer afford to operate— in Springfield or anywhere else. It went bankrupt; its gargantuan building is empty. Other companies in both Windsor and Springfield have relocated somewhat and may move out entirely within the near future.

GEORGE PERKINS MARSH

He was a scientist, philosopher, linguist, lawyer, statesman and diplomat. He also was a Vermont son. George Perkins Marsh, born in Woodstock in 1801 and a Renaissance man in the truest sense, is called the father of ecology, and his book, Man and Nature, *the "fountainhead of conservation."*

On the deforested, overgrazed hills of his native state, and in the ravaged Mediterranean where he served as U.S. Minister to Turkey and Italy, Marsh saw the havoc wrought by man's carelessness and avarice. Mountainsides, without trees to hold the soil, eroded away; rivers filled with silt and were more prone to flooding; the fertility of croplands deteriorated. Marsh's message— the first such all-encompassing pronouncement on humanity's impacts on the natural world— was that man was a part of nature, not apart from it, and could not

work against nature without disastrous consequences.

In his 1864 book, Marsh advocated thoughtful, scientifically informed land management and the protection of forests, soils, water and wildlife. His thinking helped to inspire organizers of the Adirondack Forest Preserve and the United States Forest Service. Of land already wasted, Marsh said: "If the present value of timber and land will not justify the artificial re-planting

of grounds injudiciously cleared, at least nature ought to be allowed to reclothe them with a spontaneous growth of wood."

Indeed, while governments and private citizens are realizing the importance of active land and wildlife restoration, even the far-seeing Marsh probably would be astonished at the power of benevolent neglect. Through widespread abandonment of the farming way of life, the hills of Vermont are again covered with trees. While this in itself may be seen as unfortunate, Marsh's enlightening words will hover in the shared history of Vermonters as they look to the future and "devise means for maintaining the permanence of [the forests'] relations to the fields, the meadows, and the pastures, to the rain and the dews of heaven, to the springs and rivulets with which it waters the earth."

George Perkins Marsh often is called the father of the ecology movement for his book Man and Nature, *written in 1864, which called attention to the destruction created by deforestation and overgrazing.*
VERMONT HISTORICAL SOCIETY

Above: Newfane Center in winter.
ROBERT PERRON

Far right: Horse plowing near Townshend. A team of horses cannot plow more than a few acres a day, one reason farms were smaller in the days before mechanized agriculture. GEORGE WUERTHNER

Right: Golf course at Quechee near Woodstock. JAMES RANDKLEV

Religious and Social Ideas

Perhaps the old Yankee flair for ingenuity extends beyond the merely material world. The southeast region of Vermont seems to have been endowed peculiarly with spiritual innovators, as well as mechanical ones. The founder of Mormonism, Joseph Smith, was born in Sharon in 1805. Brigham Young, perhaps the most important leader of the young Church of Jesus Christ of Latter-Day Saints, was a son of Whitingham. Whatever revelations there were in the rocky hills, Smith and Young took their inspirations elsewhere. The church eventually found and claimed its own earthly kingdom in Utah.

John Humphrey Noyes managed to make Putney the center of his religion, called Perfectionism, for nearly nine years. The utopian experiment was based in communal living— sharing work, property and, apparently, mates. Local residents tolerated Noyes' group until 1847, when they got wind of the spouse-sharing part, which they equated with good old-fashioned promiscuity. The Perfectionists fled to Oneida, New York where they fashioned the now-famous silverware, and a community that lasted for 40 more years.

The Southeast has had other progressive thinkers and doers whose ideas of humanitarianism and justice now are the unquestioned values of modern society. In 1834 Anna Hunt Marsh of New Hampshire granted $10,000 for the founding of the Brattleboro Retreat, a "hospital for the relief of insane persons." One of the first of its kind in the nation, the facility featured a dairy farm worked by the patients, a patients' newspaper, recreational facilities and therapeutic camping. The Brattleboro Retreat was the first hospital to institute attendant training. Now the largest employer in the town of Brattleboro, with more than 700 employees, the Retreat is a regional center for the treatment of psychiatric, addictive and emotional disorders.

Clarina Howard Nichols of Townshend, was a leader in the Vermont struggle for women's rights. In 1852, she was the first female to address the state legislature, when she presented a petition asking for women's suffrage in school-district elections. She also crusaded for the property rights of married women in a series of editorials published in the Windham County Democrat. Eventually her efforts were rewarded with legislation granting these rights to female Vermonters.

Progressive ideas in education also have been a tradition in Vermont. The southeast corner of the state is host to several notable institutions, among which is The Experiment in International Living in Brattleboro, an organization for worldwide student exchange and training in international issues and cultures. Marlboro College, though small in size, is well regarded for self-structured liberal arts programs and summer music festivals.

Brattleboro, serving as a regional trade center in the southern part of Windham County, is strongly influenced by the proximity of the above-mentioned schools, as well as the cluster of colleges a half-hour's drive to the south in and around Amherst, Massachusetts. It is a remarkably "hip" place for a Vermont town of its size, harboring specialty apparel shops (leather and "natural fiber" clothes), several bookstores and natural-food stores, an organic-food restaurant of region-wide renown, a wholesale natural-food distributor, and a rice-cake factory. Forward-thinking attitudes have carried

over into public enterprises well. Brattleboro's public library and recreational facilities are exceptional; its representative Town Meeting is a unique solution to a traditional— but for larger communities, inefficient— form of local government.

In the mountains, at the the western rim of the southeast region, change of another sort has transfigured highland hamlets into alpine resorts. Wilmington, Dover and Wardsboro faced the advent of the increased development in the late 1960s; their tribulations sparked the creation of Act 250, one of the most all-encompassing environmental laws ever written. While these towns continue to grow, others are newer to the game. Ludlow, at the base of Okemo Mountain Ski Area, once was a fading mill town. Today traffic congestion at the town's main crossroads regularly makes the headlines of state-wide newspapers. Londonderry, neighbor to Magic Mountain Ski Area, resists a similar fate, despite cajoling developers.

A prim home in Brattleboro reflects the economic resurgence the town has experienced as people attracted by Marlboro College, the School for International Living and the pleasant rolling hills of the region have settled in the area.
GEORGE WUERTHNER

Top: The Woodstock Inn is center-
piece for the attractive town of
Woodstock.
Bottom: Whitingham monument to
the birthplace of Brigham Young.
GEORGE WUERTHNER PHOTOS

Woodstock, like Manchester, long has held a tradition as an upper-class resort town. But even more so
than that west-side gathering place of the refined and
affluent, this aristocratic village on the Ottauquechee
River, through which Rockefeller money has flowed, is so
perfectly and scrupulously an elegant old New England
town, that it almost seems a museum piece, or a minia-
ture, Green Mountain, Williamsburg. The green is im-
maculate, shaded by graceful trees; the bustling little
shops crowd behind facades of red brick and iron-filigree
trim; the Woodstock Inn, enormous and resplendent, is
surely the monarch of all the fastidiously-kept buildings
surrounding the common.

Woodstock's popularity has exacted a price, however. The noble homes along Route 4 (the main road
through the town) reportedly are suffering structural
damage from the vibrations caused by heavy and constant traffic. In fact, the entire Route 4 corridor through
this region has become both a boon and a curse. The
state now is in the midst of a debate whether and how to
revamp the strategic east-west highway. Partial re-
routing may be the answer, but communities still off the
beaten track resist having the road through their main
streets. Meanwhile, the road has brought prosperity and
congestion to the area around Queechee Gorge and the
lower Ottauqueechee River.

THE MAPLE TREE

Acer saccharum, *the sug-
ar maple, is Vermont's state
tree. While it is widely distributed throughout Eastern
forests, it seems especially
characteristic of the Green
Mountain State— cloaking
hills and lower mountain-
sides, overarching back
roads, defining meadow
edges and springing out of
the old stone walls built
there long ago.*

*When the long process of
tapping, collecting and boiling the sap into syrup is considered, it is easy to see
why a gallon of Vermont*
*maple syrup sells for $30 or
more. Most Vermonters no
longer use horses to drag giant collecting vats through
the woods, nor do many even
hang metal buckets on the
trees these days. Plastic tub-
ing has replaced the pail,
and today multicolor hoses
festoon many a sugarbush.*

*Yet, despite the new tech-
nology and more efficient
means of collection, maple
sugaring remains a labor in-
tensive, marginally profitable
venture. Approximately 40
gallons of maple sap— the
watery, vaguely sweet liquid*

*A sugar house where the watery maple sap is boiled down to make
syrup. Forty gallons of sap make one gallon of syrup.* GEORGE WUERTHNER

that rises from the roots to the buds of the tree in early spring— is required to make one gallon of syrup. Each tree donates around 10 gallons of its sap, so that millions of trees must be tapped in order to produce the annual average of a half million or so gallons of Vermont syrup. In 1980, this worked out to 38.1 percent of the total U.S. syrup supply. However, while the Green Mountain state is consistently the number-one syrup producer, the industry is fairly unimportant in the context of the whole economy. Vermont's $10-million-a-year maple products industry accounts for only 1.8 percent of the state's agricultural income.

Maple syrup was not considered the "gourmet" item it is today until a vigorous promotion campaign by the state of Vermont— which included packaging the product in quaintly illustrated metal cans— transformed the colonists' everyday sweetener into an expensive, luxury item.

The land-use history of Vermont explains the dominance of the maple, and other northern hardwood species. Settlement clearing of Vermont's woods was followed in the mid-1800s by farm abandonment, as Yankees moved west in search of more generous agricultural land. The sun-loving white pine took hold first in the open meadows; by the early 20th century the tall, straight trees were attractive to lumbermen who clearcut them. The understory of shade-tolerant hardwood saplings were then free to surge upwards, forming the hard-wood-dominated forests we know today. On the better, well drained soils, American beech, yellow birch and the fast-growing maple were the primary species.

Maple wood has long been admired for its beauty and durability, and helped in the establishment of a strong Vermont wood products industry that produces everything from cabinets to cutting boards to clothespins. About 17 percent of the state's manufacturing labor force works in wood products. Between 1955 and 1972, sugar maple was the primary timber species in Vermont, which was cutting 40 million board feet annually. White pine subsequently succeeded sugar maple as the number one species, but Acer saccharum remains a major component of the log harvest.

Top left: In the old days buckets hung on trees were collected by horse- or ox-drawn carts. VERMONT HISTORICAL SOCIETY

Center: On spring days when days are warm but nights cool, maple trees are tapped. The larger trees pictured here can sustain five or six taps without injury, but smaller trees can only sustain one or two buckets. GEORGE WUERTHNER

Top right: David McKeighan uses a power drill to tap sugar maples. GEORGE WUERTHNER

Left: Mary McKeighan adds wood to the fire to keep sap boiling in the sugar house. Maintaining the fire is a 24-hour job that the McKeighans share. GEORGE WUERTHNER

CHAPTER NINE

NORTHEAST KINGDOM

88

Tucked up against Canada and northern New Hampshire, and bounded by the Green Mountains to the west, is Vermont's "outback." This is the Northeast Kingdom, where the roads end and the trees begin.

Reportedly, the region's name originated with Senator George Aiken, who said in a 1949 speech, "You know, this is such beautiful country up here, it ought to be called the Northeast Kingdom of Vermont." Somehow, the name captured the place perfectly. The bogs, lakes, the forested hills of spruce and birch, are reminiscent of the continental belt of boreal forest that reaches across all of Canada and north to Alaska. The white and black spruce, trees common in the sub-arctic but rare in Vermont, are found here. The Northeast Kingdom once harbored the creatures of undisturbed wilderness— caribou, lynx, marten and wolves— and still is fine moose country. To complete the portrait of this region as an outlier of the great, untamed North: it boasts the state's all-time-record low temperature: -50° F at Bloomfield on the Connecticut River.

Surprisingly, though this region is Vermont's wildest quarter, no designated wilderness, wildlife refuge or other management classification gives the land the recognition and legal sanction that it deserves. The reason for this is that the Northeast Kingdom is almost wholly in private ownership— mainly that of timber companies and other large, out-of-state corporations.

Early in this century, some 350,000 acres in the region were identified as potentially suitable for incorporation with the then-proposed Green Mountain National Forest. This idea was dropped when it was deemed more important to acquire lands in southern Vermont, which is closer to major population centers. But, today, some citizens are suggesting that the area be reconsidered for possible public acquisition.

An even more ambitious and exciting dream for the still-untamed reaches of Vermont's northeast corner is the reintroduction of those species that have been eliminated from the region's fauna. With a large enough core of protected habitat, it is conceivable that creatures such as caribou, wolves and martens could live again in the state.

De Facto Wilderness

The Kingdom remains largely de facto wilderness partly because the land— while superb for wildlife— does not encourage human prosperity. Not only is the climate severe, but also the thin soils are nutrient-poor and unproductive, and much of the area is swampy. The underlying bedrock is similar in age and structure to the White Mountains of New Hampshire— another region notoriously unsuited to agriculture. Granite forms the core of the Kingdom's undulating uplands and isolated peaks, like Burke Mountain near Lyndonville and Mt. Monadnock by Lemington.

The combination of glaciation and the region's particular rock structure produced many lakes here, more than anywhere else in Vermont. Lake Memphremagog is the state's second largest lake, although only one third of its 30-mile length actually lies south of the Canadian border. Those who must have Vermont's lakes

East of St. Johnsbury. JAMES RANDKLEV

Facing page, left: Cows graze on a spring evening near Craftsbury.

Right: The Moose River flows through the bogs and boreal forest of Victory Basin in Vermont's wildest and most remote region, which once harbored wolves, caribou and lynx. Most of this country is privately owned in large blocks by timber companies. Public acquistion of these holdings has been suggested to pave the way for wildlife reintroductions and creation of a Northeast Kingdom National Park.
GEORGE WUERTHNER PHOTOS

Top: Traffic signs in French are common near Vermont's Canadian border.
Right: Looking west toward Jay Peak from near Derby Center.
Bottom: Orleans County is considered one of the five Class 1 agricultural regions in the state, with dairying the main farm occupation.
GEORGE WUERTHNER PHOTOS

only in Vermont claim that Lake Seymour, to the southeast of Memphremagog, actually is the state's second biggest water body. Among the region's numerous other lacustrine features are Big Averill Pond, Little Averill Pond, Maidstone Lake, Norton Pond, Island Pond, Lake Willoughby, Caspian Lake, Crystal Lake, Echo Lake and a host of others.

Although many of the town charters in the region were granted in the 1760s, the harshness of the environment discouraged settlement until much later. Averill, for example, received its charter in 1762, but saw not even one resident until 1830. In its heyday, around 1880, "crowded" Averill boasted 48 citizens. Since then the number of year-round residents steadily has decreased to the present 17. The loyal townsfolk of Averill earn their way providing supplies and services to visitors who come to fish, snowmobile and hunt, in and around Big and Little Averill lakes. Lewis, the town just south of

Averill, received its charter in 1762 and never has had a single inhabitant. Lewis is almost completely in the ownership of a private timber company.

Making a living always was difficult here, and it still is. The three counties of Caledonia, Orleans and Essex are by far the poorest and most rural in the state. While cows never outnumbered people in Vermont, in many Northeast Kingdom towns moose almost certainly outnumber humans. Even Brighton, the largest town in Essex County, has only 1,545 residents. In the entire county there are 6,583 people: only a little more than 1 percent of Vermont's total population. Caledonia, Orleans and Essex counties, even taken together, all three counties are home to less than 10 percent of the state's population.

In fact, the entire county of Essex had more people in 1900 (8,048) than it does today (6,586). And not until 1980 did both Caledonia and Orleans Counties surpass their turn-of-the-century populations. As an illustration of the region's remoteness, the village of Granby did not receive electricity until 1963!

Much of the recent growth in Caledonia and Orleans counties can be attributed to migration of new residents to Newport City and Newport Town in Orleans County, which have a combined total of 6,000 people, and to St. Johnsbury in Caledonia County, with 8,000 inhabitants. These communities are becoming more important as regional trade and service centers, even while some large industries have shut down operations.

As with most of the state, total employment in farming is small. But the percentage of land area devoted to agriculture is relatively high compared to the state average, particularly in Orleans County, which has the fourth-highest density of dairy cows in the state and is one of five Class One agricultural counties. The numerous farms in Orleans give the western side of this region an open, pastoral character similar to that of the Champlain Lowlands. At the opposite extreme are towns in Essex County, like Lewis, Ferdinand and Brunswick, that have few or no farms and are almost entirely tree-covered.

Forests Were Bad and Good

These forests support a wood-products industry that includes plywood, lumber, paper and furniture manufacturing. In Essex County, 84 percent of the manufacturing jobs are in wood-related industries. This region is the largest producer of saw logs in the state; Caledonia County leads, followed by Lamoille and Essex counties. The Northeast Kingdom also is number one in terms of pulpwood production. Essex County is first, Caledonia and Orleans follow. Many of the larger companies control their own timberlands. Champion International claims 225,000 acres, mostly in Essex County, making it the largest private landowner in the state.

Although the logging industry is important and active here, when it is compared to operations in the western states, it appears to be less devastating. The land quickly revegetates and the scars of harvest soon are masked. Because the trees grow so fast, Essex County does not appear to have been cut over repeatedly— as it has been. What little original settlement was seen here was related to the logging boom of the late 1800s, when lumber camps dotted the now almost deserted woods. Victory, for example, which now claims fewer than 60 residents, once bragged of 600 inhabitants during the 1890s.

Above: A stone fence lines the only road through the hamlet of Granby in isolated Essex County.

Left: Lake Willoughby's U-shaped profile and fjord-like appearance are results of glaciers that once flowed through its valley.
GEORGE WUERTHNER PHOTOS

Above: The Moose River flows through the nearly unpeopled boreal forests of the Northeast Kingdom.
Right: New shoots grow up through last year's dead grasses in Victory Bog.

Facing page: A baseball game on the Craftsbury Common signals the approach of summer.
GEORGE WUERTHNER PHOTOS

The forests of the Northeast Kingdom today are considered an asset, but to the first travelers they presented an immense obstacle. During the Revolutionary War period, American military leaders feared that if the Lake Champlain travel corridor were cut off, there would be no reasonable access between the colonies and Canada. To provide an alternative to the Champlain waterway, in 1776 the Continental Congress approved the construction of a military highway, which was eventually known as the Bayley-Hazen Road for its two major proponents. The road began at Newbury on the Connecticut River and was to have terminated at St. John, Quebec. However, construction never progressed farther north than Hazen's Notch near Westfield.

The area's first tourist attractions were not the lakes and woods that today draw enthusiastic visitors, but instead the mineral springs that were credited with curing all sorts of ailments. The development of these springs in the northeast corner depended, especially in this remote region, on ready railroad access. Waters with a foul odor or taste were the best kind of medicine, according to health aficionados of the Victorian era.

The spring waters at Wheelock were attractive for their sulphur content; they tasted like rotten eggs. The Brunswick Mineral Springs on the Connecticut River perhaps were the best known of these therapeutic waters. A.J. Congden, the owner of the springs, assigned a different name to each of six different natural fountains. One was named Iron Spring, another Calcium Spring; number six was called Arsenic Spring. By combining varying amounts of water from each of these six taps, Congden claimed that most human afflictions could be

Newport, located partially on glacial moraines that dam the waters of 33-mile-long Lake Memphremagog, once was a lumber-producing center. Although still supporting a timber industry, it has diversified its economy with manufacturing and tourism. GEORGE WUERTHNER

cured. Whether the Brunswick Springs actually cured anyone is not documented, but business was brisk and people flocked to the resort.

The mineral springs have fallen out of style, but the Northeast Kingdom still has its vacation devotees. The "hunting camp"—a small cabin or shack used but once a year during the deer season—is a Vermont institution, sprinkled liberally in the region's backwoods. The "summer camps" are cottages and cabins, usually sited on beautiful lakeshores like those of Lakes Willoughby, Caspian, Seymour, Memphremagog and Maidstone. Towns like Newport do a brisk business each year with the influx of fair-weather Vermonters.

It used to be that summer or autumn were the only tourist seasons, but ski development at Burke Mountain and Jay Peak, as well as the popularity of snowmobiling and cross-country skiing, have breathed new life into the recreation and visitor service industry. Jay Peak ski resort is owned by a group of Montreal businessmen and caters primarily to a French-Canadian clientele, which

Newport, both a city and a town, has a combined population of 6,000, and is situated on a sloping promontory along the southern end of glacially-carved Lake Memphremagog. Part of the city is built on moraine deposited by the retreating glaciers. Lake Memphremagog, which means "beautiful waters" in the language of the Abenaki Indians, once was part of a major north-south Indian canoe route between the St. Lawrence drainage and the Connecticut River. During the French and Indian War this natural pathway through the wilderness saw hostile parties from both sides go up and down, between New England and Canada, to raid villages in enemy territory.

The town was first chartered as Duncansboro and was not settled until 1793. The forests were thick and dense; carving out a farm was a long, tedious project. In 1800, there were approximately 50 hardy souls residing along the lake, growing potatoes and other farm products. With the general logging boom of the 19th century, Newport became a lumber-mill and shipping center. Logs choked the bay

and the saws at the Prouty and Miller lumber mill—at one time the largest lumber company east of the Mississippi—were operating day and night.

Given the town's strategic position on the railway routes—as the southern terminus of the Quebec Central Railroad, and as a Canadian Pacific station on the mail line between Montreal and Boston—the railroad understandably joined the lumber mills as the backbone of the economy.

After the big logging and railroad days, Newport began to promote its attractiveness as a recreation center. With skating, ice fishing, snowmobiling, and skiing at nearby Jay Peak in winter, and boating, fishing, sailing and swimming in the summer; as well as the busy weeks of foliage and deer-

hunting seasons, the Newport area is an outdoor enthusiast's paradise. The winter season is celebrated during the annual Winterfest, which includes an international dogsled race, "sno-golf" tournaments, and a triathlon of skating, cross-country skiing and snowshoeing. In summer there is the Aquafest celebration, which features a 27-mile endurance swim from Newport to Magog, Quebec.

Newport is not dependent solely upon the tourist trade. Manufacturing also is part of the diverse local economy. Ski wear is manufactured at Slalom Ski Wear and Bogner Industries; plywood manufacturing occurs at Columbia Plywood, plastics are made at Newport Plastics, and precision tool work takes place at Thibodeau Machine Company.

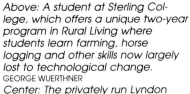

Above: A student at Sterling College, which offers a unique two-year program in Rural Living where students learn farming, horse logging and other skills now largely lost to technological change. GEORGE WUERTHNER

Center: The privately run Lyndon Academy provides for the educational needs of local high school students as well as non-residents from around the country. The town is also home to Lyndon State College. GEORGE WUERTHNER

Right: Fiddle contest at Craftsbury Common. FRANK BALTHIS

makes up 80 percent of the patrons. With Montreal less than a two-hour drive away and a lack of significant peaks in Quebec, Jay Peak has become a favorite ski resort of Canadians. Burke Mountain offers not only skiing, but also, like many high peaks in Vermont, a scenic toll road to the top, open in summer. Splendid views of the entire region and the nearby White Mountains of New Hampshire can be had here.

Waves of Immigrants

Most settlers of the Kingdom were New England Yankees, but the towns of Ryegate and Barnet were established by Scots, who immigrated to America with the express purpose of settling in Vermont. In 1773, two Scots, James Whitelaw and David Allen, traveled extensively throughout the colonies looking for an appropriate location for a new town. After seeing the Ryegate region, they bought about half the original grant from Reverend John Witherspoon, then president of Princeton University. The outbreak of the Revolution slowed the settlement of the town, but after the war the Scottish farmers moved to their new lands. When Caledonia County was formed in 1792, it was given the old Roman name for Scotland.

These early Scottish settlers were interested primarily in farming, but the granite quarries of the late 1800s brought a new wave of Scots to Vermont. Skilled stonecutters found ready employment. In fact the immigrant Scotsmen soon came to own most of the granite quarries in northern Vermont, including those at Ryegate, Kirby and East Haven. Hardwick was the stone-cutting center for the nearby Woodbury quarries, from which was taken the stone for the Chicago Court House, the Navy Memorial at Vicksburg and the Pennsylvania Capitol.

Many French Canadians came to work in the granite quarries also. They found employment, too, as farm laborers, loggers and mill workers. As in the Lake Champlain area, this ethnic group still constitutes a large proportion of the population. All of the towns lining the Canadian border in the Northeast Kingdom have 30 percent or more residents who claim French-Canadian heritage.

ST. JOHNSBURY

St. Johnsbury is a factory town in the true sense of the term, yet it bears little resemblance to the run-down, mono-architectural communities one typically envisions. From its early days, it has been dominated by one industry, and one family, whose name was Fairbanks.

Located at the confluence of three rivers, the Passumpsic, Moose and Sleepers, St. Jay, as it is affectionately called, was settled early by the Fairbanks family, who operated a store and small mill. In 1823, Thaddeus Fairbanks, an inventor and wagon builder by trade, opened a foundry to manufacture a wood stove and a cast iron plow of his own design. Thaddeus, along with his brother Erastus, decided to expand the business to include the manufacture of hemp rope. The brothers bought their hemp by the wagonload, but had a difficult time weighing their orders accurately. This prompted Thaddeus to devise a new weighing machine in 1830. Although the rope business soon foundered, demand for Thaddeus's scales mushroomed and the Fairbanks Scale Company was born.

Above: A worker puts together a computerized scale at the Fairbanks Scale Company, founded in 1830 in St. Johnsbury by the Fairbanks brothers and still the most important employer in town.
Right: Striking Victorian architecture is one feature of St. Johnsbury, a railroad center and industrial town whose ornate public buildings are the legacy of Fairbanks family. GEORGE WUERTHNER PHOTOS

Prior to Fairbanks' invention, there was no accurate or easy way to weigh large loads such as a wagon of hay. Thaddeus, using a series of levers, was able to reduce the weight necessary to counterbalance a load. The new scale was an immediate success and the Fairbanks Scale Company went on to produce scales that could weigh items as light as postal letters or as heavy as 500-ton freight barges. The new company was enormously successful— by 1882, it was producing 80,000 scales a year. Fairbanks Scales now has been operating in St. Johnsbury for more than 150 years— although the company today is owned and operated by Colt Industries.

The Fairbanks family amassed a sizable fortune from their business, and used a great deal of the money to shape St. Johnsbury into their vision of the ideal community. One lasting act of their largess was the establishment of the St. Johnsbury Academy in 1842 to provide "intellectual, moral and religious training for their own children and the children of the community." The academy still is operating and the town sends all of its children to the private high school. The sound education the students receive here is evidenced by the relatively high number of graduates who go on to college. Some 70 percent continue their education after graduation from the academy.

In 1871, in the continuing effort to encourage learning among St. Jay children, Horace Fairbanks built the St. Johnsbury Athenaeum. The centerpiece of the gallery is Albert Bierstadt's painting, "The Domes of Yosemite," purchased for $10,000 at a New York art auction.

The Fairbanks family also built the Fairbanks Museum of Natural History, which is filled with a collection of stuffed birds and animals from around the world, as well as artifacts from Africa, Oceania and South America. The museum also houses a planetarium.

Today St. Johnsbury is the regional trade center for the Northeast Kingdom and still is the home of Fairbanks Scales company. Although St. Johnsbury has lost several major businesses, other companies such as the St. Johnsbury Trucking Company, one of the largest freight hauling companies in the nation, and the EHV Weidmann Industries, which manufactures High Voltage Transformers, keep the town alive and vibrant. St. Jay residents have plenty of good reasons to stay just where they are.

CHAPTER TEN

CENTRAL REGION

Flat land is at a premium in the three counties—Washington, Orange and Lamoille—that make up the region of Central Vermont. The Green Mountains preside on the westward edge; the rolling hill country of the Vermont Piedmont controls the east half, where even more vertical relief is provided by several prominent, parallel ridges such as the Northfield and Worcester Mountains. Only at Orange County's eastern border, where the Connecticut River winds peaceably along, is a respectable expanse of lowland reached.

Montpelier and Barre, the region's two largest communities, are graphic testimonials to the scarcity of level ground. Having outgrown the narrow river valley in which they germinated, the towns' business districts are strung along the Winooski and its tributaries. Residential areas sweep up the surrounding hills like nets of ivy growing over a wall. In fact, except for the Connecticut River settlements, most of the towns in this region lie on upland slopes or along the upper reaches and feeder streams of the Winooski, the Lamoille and the White Rivers. The generally high elevation of Central Vermont communities, with Randolph Center at 1,384', Corinth Corners at 1,507', and East Topsham at 1,018' above sea level, is seen as an advantage by some who claim it brings them closer to God and heaven.

Although locals may curse the hilly terrain when the roads are covered with ice and snow, the hills and peaks have brought much of the region's wealth and fame. From its early history, this area has produced valuable commodities from its rocks and minerals. In the 1800s, salt was taken from the mountain just behind the state capitol in Montpelier, while granite was quarried at Barre, Topsham, Randolph, Cabot, Calais and Williamstown. Talc and asbestos were mined at Johnson and Belvidere. While many of these operations have closed down, Vermont still is a leading producer of granite and asbestos (second in the nation) and of talc (third largest total production in the U.S.). A more recently exploited resource is the land itself, capitalized upon and developed for the ski industry, second homes and tourism. Ski resorts line the corridor between Sugarbush near Waitsfield and Warren, to Mt. Mansfield and Spruce Mountain by Stowe.

Despite the rural look of most of the region, the heart of Central Vermont lies in the sister cities of Montpelier and Barre. Although only five miles apart, they are startlingly different. The state capital is sited at Montpelier, where sharp-looking professionals and legislators in coats and ties walk in march-step along the well-kept, prosperous main street. Barre, home of the largest granite quarries in the state, is a blue-collar town and bears a care-worn but still-proud appearance.

Barre was given its name by a native of Barre, Massachusetts in 1793. The town had been chartered as Wildersburgh, but the townspeople felt it sounded "uncouthly." Two residents each wished to give the names of their hometowns in Massachusetts to the settlement, and agreed that the winner of a wrestling duel between them would have the honor of renaming Wildersburgh. Jonathan Sherman and "Barre" were the winners.

Today Barre is the name of both a city and a town. Like Rutland and Newport, the city was carved from the original town and became an independent political en-

The Mad River Valley. FRANK BALTHIS

Facing page, right: East Corinth on an October morning is typical of the many picturesque villages that dot the rolling country of central Vermont. JEFF GNASS

Left: At Manchester Lumber in Johnson. The early sawmills cut primarily white pine, but today most Vermont sawmills produce hardwood lumber for furniture, paneling and other uses. GEORGE WUERTHNER

tity. Barre City was created from Barre town in 1894 and has one of the highest population densities in the state with more than 2,500 people per square mile. Near the turn of the century the city bustled with the activity of skilled artisans, carving the granite blocks into beautiful statues and monuments. At one time more than 3,500 granite cutters lived in Barre City, but as in many other industries, technological advances and changes in demand have resulted in a sharp decline in the number of employees needed to take the rock through the process, from rough-cut blocks to finished objects.

Unlike Burlington or other Vermont communities that have seen a large influx of out-of-staters, a substantial majority of Barre residents— 79 percent— are native Vermonters. By contrast, only 40 percent of the inhabitants of Fayston, a ski-resort town in the Mad River Valley, are Vermont-born. Another feature of Barre's blue-collar heritage is the relatively low fraction of college-educated citizens— just 11 percent. In Fayston, 40 percent of the adult residents have college degrees.

Granite quarrying began here shortly after the War of 1812, but the industry remained small due to the great cost and logistical difficulties of transporting the massive blocks of stone. Without access to viable transport, the rock did not travel far. However, after construction of the Montpelier and Barre Railroad (formerly the Barre and Chelsea) in the 1880s, granite building blocks were readily carried to out-of-state markets. It is the steepest standard-gauge railroad east of the Rockies.

This linking of the Barre quarries to the outside world brought with it a dramatic increase in production, as well as population. From 2,100 residents in 1880, the town leaped to a population of 6,812 people in 1890. This was the greatest level of growth ever experienced by a single Vermont town. Buoyed by a flood of immigrants, mostly stone-cutters and quarry workers from overseas, Barre's population continued to grow until it reached more than 12,000 by 1910. The new citizens came in waves from different nations. In 1890, one out of every five Barre residents was Scottish. By 1910, more than 14 percent of the townsfolk claimed Italy as their birthplace. Today French-Canadians are the largest minority, and people descended from this ethnic group made up more than 40 percent of Barre's inhabitants in 1980.

Dozens of granite quarries have been opened in Vermont at one time or another, but the largest actively operating quarry is at the Rock of Ages pit near Graniteville. It is more than 100 years old, is 350' deep and occupies some 20 acres. Eighty-five percent of the rock removed from the quarry is discarded because of imper-

fections, so that only 15 percent is retained as monument stone.

The original method of removal was to blast the granite from the hillside, but much of the stone shattered in the process. Today granite is broken away by drilling a series of parallel holes along a line, eventually leaving a clean cut called a channel. Another method involves rapidly heating the rock along the desired channel. This causes the stone to expand and flake off, whereupon small holes are drilled beneath the block, and black-powder charges are used to crack it loose. The granite piece then is hoisted from the quarry and trucked to the stone sheds where workmen cut out, smooth and polish the rock, and engrave the finished monuments.

In the infant years of the granite industry, about half the rock was used for building stone, but its popularity in this capacity has declined so that the majority of

granite now quarried ends up as gravestones, or "monuments" as the industry prefers to call them. To see a sample of the old-style building stone, one need go no farther than the Vermont Statehouse in Montpelier. The present capitol is the third to have been built. The first statehouse was constructed in 1808, but was torn down because it was considered too small. The second building was made of Barre granite, one of the first projects ever to utilize the locally-obtained stone. It was completed in 1838. This structure burned in 1857 and only the granite columns and walls survived the flames.

Today the edifice crowned with a gold-leaf dome and fronted by an open, grassy lawn gives Montpelier a graceful, stately look that Barre lacks. However, beyond the verdant open space granted to Vermont's capitol, Montpelier looks more like a gangly kid who has outgrown his clothes. The city seems to flow over the walls of the narrow Winooski valley. Those unfortunate

Above: Covered bridge and pond at Warren, located near Sugarbush ski area, where a large percentage of land and housing is owned by non-residents. FRANK BALTHIS

Left: The first state capitol was constructed in 1808 but torn down and replaced in 1838 with a larger building that utilized Barre granite. This second structure burned in 1857 and was replaced by the present building. GEORGE WUERTHNER

Facing page: Ornate granite monument in the famous Hope Cemetery in Barre where many stone cutters are buried. GEORGE WUERTHNER

Above: A flea market in Waterbury. Located halfway between Burlington and Montpelier, Waterbury has seen a resurgence as a bedroom community for professionals working in state government or high-tech industries. JOHN LYNCH

Right: IMAGERY

enough to be in need of a parking space during the legislative session will vouch for Montpelier's dearth of elbow room.

Nevertheless, the cozy town of 8,000, cupped like a robin's egg in a nest of gentle, forested hills, is the smallest and likely the most livable state capital in the country. With more than 1,000 people directly employed by the government, it is one of the most completely white-collar towns in the state. Montpelier also is the region's economic hub, and employs a greater number of workers than the total of town residents. As the center of Green Mountain law-making, Montpelier has the dubious distinction of counting more attorneys per capita than any other community in the nation.

Outside Montpelier and Barre, the central region's inhabitants are spread out among many small villages and rural farms. One of the fastest-growing areas is in the western portion where the ski resorts of Sugarbush, Sugarbush North and Mad River Glen have brought economic boom times, as well as development headaches to the towns of the Mad River Valley. In 1960, the permanent population of Warren was 469, Waitsfield stood at 658 and Fayston had 158 residents, but by 1985, these same towns had 1,019, 1,404, and 738 people respectively. The grand list in Warren rocketed from $6 million in 1960 to $451 million by 1976. Fayston has had a 367 percent growth rate during the past 10-year period! Not surprisingly, the percentages of residents born outside Vermont in such towns— Fayston (60 percent), Waitsfield (52 percent), and Warren (60 percent)— are exceptionally high. These communities also are owned by a large proportion of out-of-staters: Warren, 54 percent non-Vermont ownership, Fayston, 49 percent. For comparison, only 1 percent of Barre City is owned by non-residents.

Older than the Mad River ski areas, the Stowe region has been a tourist mecca for more than a hundred years. Its attractiveness is attributable to its proximity to Vermont's highest peak, 4,393' Mt. Mansfield. The mountain's long ridge is said by some to resemble the profile of an upturned human face, hence, the Chin (a jutting ledge), and the Nose (the highest rocky pinnacle). In 1858, a hotel was built just below the Nose and was accessed by a carriage road. Among the summit house's most famous guests, Ralph Waldo Emerson was a particular admirer of the scenery, and proclaimed the view of Lake Champlain to the west a "perpetual illusion."

Its reputation as a resort helped to establish Stowe as one of the first ski areas in the country. Ski trails were cut on Mt. Mansfield and a rope tow was installed by the Civilian Conservation Corps in 1933; the first chair lift was constructed in 1940. At one time Stowe was unchallenged as the ski destination of the East. Downhill skiing is not the only winter activity, for gliding through the woods on a pair of "skinny skis" also is popular in the Stowe area.

Waterbury sits squarely between Stowe and the Mad River Valley resort communities. It also lies in the busy east-west corridor that connects Burlington and Montpelier. Long a crossroads town, Waterbury also once was the home of the state mental hospital. The extensive brick facilities now house a number of state agencies that outgrew their accommodations in Montpelier. The immigration of the government offices and the accessibility of Waterbury to both the Queen City and the capital has meant a burgeoning population of young, professional residents, and an accompanying renaissance of the downtown area.

Waterbury has also become the lucky host of Ben and Jerry's Ice Cream, a company founded on a whim by two young entrepreneurs, Ben Cohen and Jerry Greenfield. In 1978, they completed a $5 correspondence course on ice cream making and opened a shop in an old gas station in Burlington. The popularity of their product, however, soon sent them looking for a new home. The partners' success stems from two things: using the very best ingredients and, even more importantly, a sense of fun. No doubt, the appealing idea of "pure Vermont milk and eggs" also wins customers.

The company founders— both products of the socially-minded '60s— believe that businesses should be responsible to the communities that host them. One of their first actions was to offer company stock to Vermont residents; as the company thrived, so would Vermonters. In addition, the company created a non-profit foundation that donates thousands of dollars each year to local organizations and causes. Ben and Jerry also decreed that the highest-paid employee cannot make more than five times the wages of the lowest-paid worker.

Vermont Castings Company of Randolph enjoyed a similarly phenomenal rise to fortune and success. Founded by three young partners in 1975, the company had 400 employees by 1983. Today it is one of the largest employers in the Randolph area. Its rapid growth can be attributed to a high-quality product and the increasing popularity of wood heat. Originally, the business bought cast iron parts from foundries in Kentucky, Pennsylvania and even Germany and Holland. The partners eventually decided that the great demand for the stoves warranted the construction of their own

Above: The new Trapp Family Lodge was founded by the Von Trapp family, the subject of the play "The Sound of Music." The lodge, located at Vermont's oldest ski resort community—Stowe—caters to tourists in all seasons. Cross-country skiing on the resort's many groomed trails is one of the most popular attractions. Left: Robert Houghton of Marshfield earns his living providing split wood for wood-stove heating.
GEORGE WUERTHNER PHOTOS

Above: Store in Jeffersonville.
GEORGE WUERTHNER

Facing page: Howeacres Farm near Tunbridge on an autumn afternoon.
JEFF GNASS

computer-controlled foundry in Randolph. This was the first foundry built in the United States to produce stove plate since the turn of the century.

As with Ben and Jerry's Ice Cream, the Vermont Castings Company likes to think of its customers as part of a big family and annually hosts an "owners' party," which sometimes attracts as many as 10,000 people.

Many of the smaller communities in Central Vermont depend primarily on one industry. Northfield, south of Montpelier, once was a bustling railroad center— apparently due to the efforts of Charles Paine, one-time Vermont governor and it seems, swindler and con artist as well. When the Vermont Central Railroad was being constructed, Paine made sure it passed through Northfield instead of the more logical route through Barre, Montpelier and Williamstown Gap, where the grade was lower. The first railroad shops were built in Northfield, bringing prosperity to the town and, by no mere coincidence, to Paine also. The self-serving conniver eventually was run out of town and the railroad shops were moved to St. Albans.

Northfield, however, survived because of Norwich University, which was founded in Norwich, Vermont in 1820 and moved to its present location in 1867. It bills itself as the oldest military college in the country. While

attending Norwich, cadets follow a life of strict military discipline. Some 50 percent of the graduates enter the armed forces, and among the 44 undergraduate majors are defense studies and military science, although the college offers such traditional courses as education and business.

At the other end of the educational spectrum, Goddard College in Plainfield nurtures free thinking and self-directed learning. Feminist— not defense— studies and environmental— not military— sciences are part of the curriculum. One may even earn a degree from Goddard when not at Goddard: the off-campus degree program is a chance to pursue academic inquiry outside the confines of school walls and rigid requirements.

Johnson State College lies somewhere between Goddard and Norwich on the scale of educational regimentation. Placed on a high hill overlooking the Lamoille River Valley and Mount Mansfield, this attractive, small institution was founded in 1828 as a grammar school for the children of Johnson town. Johnson State gradually evolved into a four-year college that today offers coursework in fields ranging from elementary education to environmental sciences.

In a number of ways, Johnson's economy mirrors that of many other small Vermont communities. There is the major employer— the college, in Johnson's case— and there are the local businesses serving the needs of the townspeople: the town cafe, the local food store. In addition, Johnson has a number of small companies, including the Manchester Lumber Mill, the Vermont Talc Company— which mills and processes talc ore— and Butternut Tree Farm, which produces Christmas trees and maple syrup for sale in the farm store, as well as for distribution throughout the region.

Although the town of Johnson hardly is a bustling metropolis, it seems a cosmopolitan place indeed when compared with hill-and-dale communities like East Corinth, East Topsham and Tunbridge. These and other handkerchief-sized hamlets, with little more than a general store and post office, subsist— one surmises— on a few lost tourists and some very unhurried commerce. Despite their humble size and minuscule contribution to the state gross product, however, these towns— barely more than chance clusterings of buildings tucked in between the hills— give the region its characteristic charm.

In a sense, Central Vermont is a mirror of all of Vermont. It contains a little of each other sub-region, with ski resorts, urban centers, dairy farms, rock quarries and spruce-pine forests. In essence, this is Vermont as Vermonters think of their state.

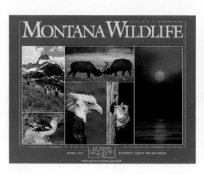
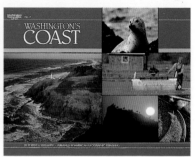